Sleuthing the Alamo

New Narratives in American History

Series Editors
James West Davidson
Michael B. Stoff

Sleuthing the Alamo

DAVY CROCKETT'S LAST STAND AND
OTHER MYSTERIES OF THE TEXAS REVOLUTION

JAMES E. CRISP

North Carolina State University

NEW YORK   OXFORD
OXFORD UNIVERSITY PRESS
2005

Oxford University Press

Oxford   New York
Auckland   Bangkok   Buenos Aires   Cape Town   Chennai
Dar es Salaam   Delhi   Hong Kong   Istanbul   Karachi   Kolkata
Kuala Lumpur   Madrid   Melbourne   Mexico City   Mumbai   Nairobi
São Paulo   Shanghai   Taipei   Tokyo   Toronto

Copyright © 2005 by Oxford University Press, Inc.

Published by Oxford University Press, Inc.,
198 Madison Avenue, New York, New York 10016
www.oup.com

Oxford is a registered trademark of Oxford University Press

Library of Congress Cataloging-in-Publication Data

Crisp, James E., 1946–
    Sleuthing the Alamo : Davy Crockett's last stand and other mysteries of
the Texas Revolution / by James E. Crisp.
        p. cm.—(New narratives in American history)
    Includes bibliographical references.
    ISBN 0-19-516349-4 (acid-free paper)—ISBN 0-19-516350-8 (pbk. :
acid-free paper)
        1. Alamo (San Antonio, Tex.)—Siege, 1836. 2. Alamo (San Antonio,
Tex.)—Siege, 1836—Historiography. 3. Texas—History—Revolution,
1835–1836. 4. Texas—History—Revolution, 1835–1836—Historiography.
5. Texas—History—Revolution, 1835–1836—Biography. I. Title. II.
Series.

F30.C79 2004
976.4'03—dc22   2004049255

Printing number: 9 8 7 6 5 4 3 2

Printed in the United States of America
on acid-free paper

To the memory of my mother and father—
who made it all possible

CONTENTS

Color plates appear after page 174.

FOREWORD

IN MATTERS OF PROFESSIONAL ETIQUETTE, MOST HISTORIANS believe that it is far better to be heard than seen. The historian's *voice*—magisterial, judicious, assured—pervades traditional narratives and sets their tone. It tells the tale of others with proper distance from them. As for the historian's *own* history—his or her upbringing, personal predilections and passions—that remains well concealed behind the prose, except perhaps for a few words in the preface. Such an approach makes sense. The subject matter, after all, is the history, not the historian.

But in this riveting study of the Texas Revolution, James E. Crisp not only breaks the rules of etiquette but tramples them front to back. He makes himself a central character in this narrative, beginning with his own West Texas upbringing in the small town of Henrietta. There he was exposed to the myths of Texas history through a remarkable series of cartoons, misleadingly titled *Texas History Movies*, assigned to students all across the state. And in the chapters that follow, as Crisp moves on to untangle many of the myths of the Texas Revolution, he is seen *and* heard. How could Sam Houston, Crisp asks, have rallied Texan troops with the overtly racist speech found in his official papers, when he had lived happily with the Cherokee Indians as both a youth and an adult? Like a seasoned gumshoe, Crisp follows a trail of evidence that leads from San Antonio to Germany and back, from mistranslated manuscripts to censored children's books to Houston's papers themselves.

How did the legendary Davy Crockett die at the Alamo? Instead of a straight-on account of those final hours, Crisp takes us through a different sort of hand-to-hand combat, debating the evidence for Crockett's summary execution with a dogged, former arson detective and fielding hate mail from defenders of Davy's legend.

In the end, there is good reason for the historian *not* to disappear behind a veil of measured prose. As Crisp points out time after time, some voices of the Texas Revolution have been placed in the limelight, while others have been neglected or even silenced. We cannot understand the reasons for the silencing unless we witness the process by which the history of the Revolution has been manufactured over the previous two centuries and until we observe, through Crisp's own story, how that heritage continues to be fought over to this day. Such an unorthodox tale makes a worthy addition to the Oxford New Narratives in American History, a series that looks to push the boundaries of both traditional historical narratives and methods.

James West Davidson
Michael B. Stoff
Series Editors

ACKNOWLEDGMENTS

SLEUTHING THE ALAMO IS A DISTILLATION OF MY SCHOLARLY work in all its facets over more than a decade. Any list of those who have provided assistance along the way would inevitably omit the names of people to whom I am deeply grateful. Though many of these people are mentioned in the text, the others should know that my heartfelt gratitude extends to them as well.

Without the encouragement of two very special friends and mentors, however, this book would not exist. Ron Tyler, Director of the Texas State Historical Association, has provided critical support at every juncture, repeatedly turning dead ends into unexpected opportunities. I have not forgotten that I owe him another book.

James W. Davidson, my series editor at Oxford University Press, has been a source of intellectual inspiration since the day we began graduate school together in 1968. It has been a precious gift to have an editor who knows me better than I know myself.

CHRONOLOGY

Major Events of the Texas Revolution,

Autumn 1835–Spring 1836

OCTOBER 2: THE BATTLE OF GONZALES Anglo-American settlers repulse a Mexican force sent from San Antonio de Béxar to seize a cannon held by the citizens of Gonzales.

OCTOBER 10: THE CAPTURE OF GOLIAD Texan volunteers seize the Goliad presidio on the San Antonio River, cutting off the supply line from the sea to General Cos and his Mexican force at San Antonio.

OCTOBER 28: THE BATTLE OF CONCEPCIÓN Texan and Mexican forces clash at the Concepción Mission south of San Antonio. Mexican losses are heavy, Texan light.

OCTOBER 28–DECEMBER 4: THE SIEGE OF BÉXAR Rebel Texan forces, joined by Tejanos and a few Mexican Federalists, surround and bombard Mexican troops in San Antonio and the nearby Alamo.

NOVEMBER 1–14: THE CONSULTATION Delegates from across Texas meet at San Felipe de Austin and declare conditional loyalty to the Mexican Federalist Constitution of 1824.

DECEMBER 5–9: THE STORMING OF BÉXAR   The Texans attack San Antonio and force the surrender of General Cos and his forces after days of house-to-house fighting. Cos is allowed to withdraw from Texas with his troops.

DECEMBER 30: THE MATAMOROS EXPEDITION BEGINS Colonel Frank W. Johnson and Dr. James Grant lead the majority of Texan soldiers out of San Antonio toward Goliad and Refugio, with the avowed goal of pushing across the Río Grande to the city of Matamoros. The Alamo is left with few supplies and barely one hundred men.

JANUARY 18–FEBRUARY 8:   James Bowie, William Barret Travis, and David Crockett each arrive at the Alamo, but bring relatively few reinforcements with them.

FEBRUARY 23: THE SIEGE OF THE ALAMO BEGINS General Santa Anna and a large Mexican force arrive suddenly in San Antonio and lay siege to fewer than two hundred Texans barricaded in the Alamo. The siege will last into the thirteenth day.

FEBRUARY 27–MARCH 2: THE MATAMOROS EXPEDITION ENDS   Johnson's and Grant's forces are surprised and destroyed near the Nueces River by a Mexican force under General José Urrea. Johnson escapes, but almost all of the Texans die, including Grant.

MARCH 1–17: THE CONVENTION   Meeting at Washington-on-the-Brazos, Texan delegates declare the independence of the Republic of Texas on March 2, 1836.

MARCH 6:   The Alamo falls after an early-morning assault by Mexican forces commanded by Santa Anna. The defenders are wiped out.

MARCH 11–13:   Texan General Sam Houston arrives in Gonzales, where he learns of the fall of the Alamo. He begins a long eastward retreat as Mexican forces pursue him.

MARCH 20:   Colonel James W. Fannin and most of his command are captured while attempting to retreat from Goliad by Mexican forces under General Urrea.

MARCH 27:   Fannin and over four hundred of his men are executed at Goliad on the explicit orders of Santa Anna.

MARCH 31–APRIL 12:   Sam Houston rests and drills his army near the plantation of Jared Groce on the Brazos River above San Felipe de Austin.

APRIL 12:   Santa Anna's forces begin crossing the Brazos at Thompson's Ferry, below San Felipe de Austin. Houston's army begins crossing the Brazos at Groce's Landing.

APRIL 20:   Santa Anna and an advance guard of fewer than a thousand men set up camp barely a mile from Sam Houston's nine-hundred-man army near Lynch's Ferry on the San Jacinto River; mild skirmishing occurs during the day.

APRIL 21:   Santa Anna is reinforced by four hundred more troops from the Brazos River; no fighting occurs until late afternoon, when Houston's men suddenly attack, killing half of Santa Anna's men and capturing most of the remainder. Santa Anna is captured the following day.

APRIL 23: The Mexican forces in Texas, now under the command of General Vicente Filisola, begin a withdrawal from eastern Texas that turns into a disaster when rains turn the Texas prairies to mud. By June, most of the Mexican forces have reached Matamoros on the Río Grande.

Sleuthing the Alamo

Texas at the Time of the Revolution (1835–1836)

PRIDE AND PREJUDICE

A Personal Prologue

THE FIRST HISTORICAL FACT THAT I REMEMBER LEARNING AS A child was that the place I called home was once an independent nation. As I ritually memorized (as all Texan children do) the six flags that had flown over Texas, my mother explained to me that the Lone Star banner of what was then the biggest state in the Union had also been, more than a century before, the flag of an even bigger Republic of Texas. I thought this was cool, and I also sensed that it was somehow important.

I was born a Texan. The meaning of that identity was shaped by the constant invocation of "our" heroic struggle for freedom from a brutish oppressor—"Remember the Alamo!" Texas had been a country separate from the United States, with its own defining revolutionary experience. Mexico, not Britain, had been the enemy. The iconic heroes of the Texas Revolution were all around me, in the names of our streets and schools, our cities and counties: Houston, Austin, Fannin, Travis, Bowie, Crockett.

As a third-grader, when the Disney-inspired "Davy Crockett craze" swept the country in 1955, I was mesmerized by actor Fess Parker's portrayal of Crockett's last stand at the Alamo. A picnic table flipped on its side was all the fortress I needed to reen-

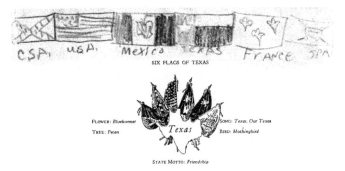

SIX FLAGS OF TEXAS

FLOWER: *Bluebonnet*

TREE: *Pecan*

Texas

SONG: *Texas, Our Texas*

BIRD: *Mockingbird*

STATE MOTTO: *Friendship*

(COPYRIGHT: TEXAS STATE HISTORICAL ASSOCIATION, AUSTIN, TEXAS.)

act that "death" a thousand times in my own backyard—the historical authenticity of the scene guaranteed by my coonskin cap and a variety of plastic weapons stamped with the magic Crockett name.

Viewers of the Disney epic on television (and in the subsequent movie) were not allowed to see Crockett overwhelmed by the bluecoats who swarmed around him at the end, and I must admit that in my backyard battles, I don't remember dying, either. Like Davy, I just kept on killing Mexicans. These were imaginary Mexicans, of course. As far as I knew, there were no "real" Mexicans in the Clay County of 1955.

I did know that there were black people in my home town of Henrietta, but my society was so deeply segregated I did not speak to an African American my own age until I was in college. Yet, by the time that the Supreme Court's 1954 *Brown v. Board of Education* decision declared the unconstitutionality of legally mandated racial segregation, I was already discovering that even my little community had been shaped in strange ways by a shadowy past.

My second-grade music teacher had transformed our class into a "rhythm band," equipped with sticks, cymbals, drums, tambourines, and sandpaper blocks. I played the bass drum. My first peek into Henrietta's other world came when the rhythm band performed in concert at the Fred Douglass School, a cabin on the edge of town where Henrietta's "Negro" children attended the first eight grades in a single room. (To attend high school, they had to travel to the next county.)

I had no idea who Fred Douglass was—and certainly no clue that Frederick Douglass was an escaped slave whose oratory and writings made him black America's most important voice for freedom and justice in the nineteenth century. At the time, I guessed that Fred Douglass might be one of those old black men that I sometimes saw walking toward the dirt roads that ran through "niggertown," a place name used by my parents and every white person I knew.

As I beat out the bass notes of the foursquare rhythms we played that day (syncopation not being a part of our repertoire), the question "why?" was beating against my own confused brow. What was going on here? Why were these people treated so differently? What power, what law, had decreed that this part of our town would play by a different set of rules than the rest of us, with all the school's grades jumbled up in the space of a small cabin? I had glimpsed something profoundly disturbing, but at age seven, I did not have the words or the courage to question the *status quo*.

FRED DOUGLASS SCHOOL
BUILDING
(Courtesy of Henrietta, Texas, Independent School District.)

A year later, when the Supreme Court's order that public school segregation be dismantled "with all deliberate speed" coincided with the Davy Crockett mania in the spring of 1955, there is no doubt that my attention was fixed on the mythic past rather than the troublesome present. Besides, Disneyland had just opened in California, and my parents had let my sister and me know that if we saved our nickels and dimes, we might be able to go there ourselves the following year.

My only recollection of the immediate impact of the *Brown* ruling on my world is a single vignette from the elementary school playground. I can still hear the voice of Frances, a rough-hewn yellow-haired girl from a "poor-white" family, as she yelled to her partner on the seesaw that she'd "sooner go to school with injuns and meskins than with niggers!"

At this point in my sheltered North Texas life, almost all of the Indians and Mexicans I had seen were of the Hollywood type, and I shrugged off her remark as so much playground fantasy. I could not imagine how any threat posed by those inoffensive kids from the Fred Douglass School could compare to what Davy Crockett faced in the form of furtive Creek warriors and the relentless minions of the Mexican dictator Santa Anna.

By the time our family Buick made it across the Southwestern deserts to California's Magic Kingdom in the summer of 1956, the Davy Crockett frenzy had run its course, and I was far more thrilled by the rockets of Tomorrowland than the rifles of Frontierland. I was also coming to realize more and more that my region's history had its dark side.

I entered a still-segregated Henrietta Junior High in the fall of 1957. As the school year opened a few hundred miles away in Arkansas, the explosive events of the Little Rock crisis over desegregation forced me to view both the past and the present with a new seriousness. I was shocked by the silhouettes of bayonets that shared the cover of my father's news magazine with the angry face of Arkansas' defiant Governor Orval Faubus.

As Governor Faubus and his allies sought to preserve their besieged institutions of racial privilege, they invoked a bitter history that was less familiar to me than the Texans' stand against the tyranny of Santa Anna. As my dad and I watched Faubus on *Meet the Press*, he declared that President Eisenhower's dispatch of Federal troops to Little Rock to enforce the Court's desegregation order would unleash a new Reconstruction "even more heinous than the Reconstruction which followed the Civil War."

I didn't know what "heinous" meant—it sounded vaguely obscene. But I did know that Faubus was referring to events in the past that I found difficult to understand, even as I was coming to appreciate their significance. I had learned that there were black people in America because of slavery. Lincoln and the victorious Union armies had defeated the Confederacy and freed the slaves, which was tacitly acknowledged to be a good thing. Texas was on the losing side, but fought valiantly.

The memories of "Black Reconstruction" may have lain heavily on the minds of many Southerners and even many Texans in the eastern part of the state, but those old resentments were not on my radar screen in the cowboy country of Clay County. When we learned about the Civil War in Texas, we learned about Southern valor, not racial politics—how Confederate Lieutenant Dick Dowling and his handful of heroes foiled a massive Union invasion fleet, and how the very last Confederates to capitulate did so down on the Río Grande, long after Robert E. Lee had given up. It was simply the heroic Alamo message *redux*, offering no clue as to how "freedom" for the slaves at the end of the war turned into "segregation" in the years that followed.

My moral confusion as to the meaning of the Civil War was exacerbated during the 1957–1958 school year by another TV version of history: *The Gray Ghost.* As I watched the intrepid and always honorable Major Mosby and his Confederates ride circles around the bumbling Federals (the series ran for thirty-nine weeks on CBS), it was hard to remember that Texas had fought on the losing side of a war that freed the slaves. Yet the rebel banner that was so stirring to me as Mosby's men carried it into the battles of the past was the same flag that could be seen on the evening news, carried by screaming, cursing crowds in Little Rock and other Southern cities as they pelted children trying to go to school.

The following year brought a measure of relief from my galloping cognitive dissonance as I turned from this troubling and ambiguous coupling of past and present to the glories of another kind of history altogether. Seventh grade was the year for Texas history and geography, taught by the stern but kindly Coach Wayne Brockman. I loved it. The intricate map-coloring assignments, which some students loathed, became my briar patch as I developed a love affair with cartography. But nothing brought me greater pleasure in Coach Brockman's class than *Texas History Movies.*

These teaching tools were not films or slides, but cartoons—wonderful, whimsical, engaging cartoons drawn by Jack Patton, with captions written by John Rosenfield, Jr., which brought the past alive for a couple of generations of Texas schoolkids. They first appeared in serialized form in the 1920s in the *Dallas Morning News*, and thanks to the Magnolia Petroleum Company (purveyors of Mobiloil and Mobilgas under the sign of the Flying Red Horse), a comic-book version was made available each year until the 1960s to virtually every seventh-grader in Texas. Today I treasure my battered 1954 edition, with its cover page still bearing my youthful pencilled version of the six flags of Texas.

Texas History Movies did not linger over awkward subjects. In my booklet of 128 pages, secession and the Civil War got a page apiece, and the end of Reconstruction, half a page. (There was nothing at all on the substance of Reconstruction.) Given that the American annexation of Texas was not shown until the end of page 123, the canonical meaning of "Texas History" becomes clear. Seventy-five pages were allotted to the settlement and winning of Texas by Anglo-Americans between 1821 and 1846, and of the preceding fifty pages, well over half were devoted to various French and American explorers, pirates, and filibusterers. Spaniards and Mexicans got very short shrift.

Nevertheless, obscure characters who would have otherwise glazed our eyes were brought to life in the tiny soap operas that we held in our hands. The following cartoon strip shows the jealous Spanish Governor Anayas of the Mexican province of Coahuila in 1714.

(COPYRIGHT: TEXAS STATE HISTORICAL ASSOCIATION, AUSTIN, TEXAS.)

The pirate Jean Lafitte was also embroiled in romance.

(Copyright: Texas State Historical Association, Austin, Texas.)

In a dozen pages devoted to Lafitte's adventures, there is not a single allusion to his extensive slave smuggling. However, *Texas History Movies* did not shy away from graphic violence, especially in the form of Mexican cruelty and butchery. The following three representative scenes are from a failed revolt against Spain in Texas in 1813, the destruction of opposition to Santa Anna's rule in 1835, and the conflict between Mexico and the Republic of Texas in the 1840s.

(Copyright: Texas State Historical Association, Austin, Texas.)

(COPYRIGHT: TEXAS STATE HISTORICAL ASSOCIATION, AUSTIN, TEXAS.)

(COPYRIGHT: TEXAS STATE HISTORICAL ASSOCIATION, AUSTIN, TEXAS.)

From among the featured Anglo-American heroes of the Texas Revolution, I was especially drawn to Sam Houston, whose biography was allotted more than a dozen precious pages of *Texas History Movies*. Houston's life had its share of romance and violence, but I was most fascinated by his long teenage sojourn with the Cherokee Indians, for reasons both intellectual and personal.

On a family pilgrimage in the mid-1950s to my paternal grandparents' old place in the Smoky Mountains (and to the homes of my cousins around Houston's own boyhood home of Maryville, Tennessee), I visited the nearby Qualla Boundary Indian Reservation in North Carolina, where I was entranced by a reproduction of Sequoyah's Cherokee syllabary. Around the same time, I overheard the family lore (later confirmed by genealogists) that some of my grandmother Crisp's ancestors were Cherokee from Great Smokies.

I admired Sam Houston's easy friendship with the Indians (which influenced his policies for the rest of his life), but I was even more impressed by his refusal to swear allegiance to the Confederacy in 1861, even though it cost him the Texas Governor's chair—a decision that earned Houston an honored place in presidential aspirant John F. Kennedy's 1956 book *Profiles in Courage.*

Another part of the Crisp family lore that I had become aware of was in the form of a fragile and precious piece of paper that my grandfather James Lafayette Crisp kept folded in his wallet. It was his father's Union army discharge certificate. In acknowledgment of my intense interest, the document was framed and hanging in my room by the time I was in high school. Especially in light of my growing sympathy with the civil rights movement (which was beginning to create some friction at our extended family reunions), I was happy to have this documentary evidence (as I saw it) of my own Southern family's nonculpability in the defense of slavery.

The summer of 1960 brought a welcome change of pace from my usual idyllic (that is, dull and hot) summers in Henrietta. My mother had decided to go back to college to get the teacher's certificate that would help finance my own (and my younger sister's) impending university educations. After a few courses at Midwestern University in Wichita Falls, which was within easy commuting distance, all that remained for her was a final summer at her *alma mater*—North Texas State University in Denton. My younger sister Judy and I tagged along.

What an adventure for a fourteen-year-old! In addition to enrolling in a couple of challenging science and math courses at the university's demonstration high school, outside the classroom I was meeting kids from all over Texas and finding within walking distance the stamp and coin shops and bookstores that were virtually nonexistent in small Texas towns like Henrietta. I was also discovering the temptations of pinball and Playboy, and generally relishing a place that seemed much further along the curve of history than Clay County.

And this advancement meant integration. Not in my high school classes—these still followed the local rules of segregation.

But North Texas State University was admitting African American undergraduates. My experience with racial integration that summer in Denton was short, sudden, and though inconsequential on the surface of things, troubling beyond words.

One of the perks of being the child of an NTSU student was the use of the university's swimming pools. On an otherwise uneventful afternoon that summer I bounced high off the springboard, dove deep into the water, and surfaced midway down the pool, shaking the water off my face. When I opened my eyes again, I found myself only about nine inches from a young black man who was also enjoying the pool.

I knew that something was wrong. I couldn't breathe properly, I was getting dizzy, and I knew that I had to get out of the pool. What I didn't know was why—and I'm not entirely sure to this day. Earlier in the summer, a failed attempt at a flip from the diving board had slapped my face into the water so violently that I couldn't see for half a minute, but the problem this time was not my entry into the water. It was the startling circumstance I found after I surfaced. I had an inexplicable, visceral feeling that one of us should not be there. Unable to speak, I wandered away feeling shaken, confused, and deeply ashamed.

This wasn't supposed to happen. By 1960 I was an "integrationist" and a budding political liberal. Yet when I found myself face-to-face with the living object of my sympathetic support, I panicked.

It was years before I told anyone about what happened that day—years before I began to understand and to resent how deeply my socialization had affected my unconscious. I was a freshman at Rice University, in Houston, before ever speaking to a black peer, and, even when this finally happened, the alarm bells were ringing in the back of my head. Jimmy Edmondson, the savvy junior with whom I shared a suite, had invited some students from virtually all-black Texas Southern University over to talk to a few of us about the impending integration of undergraduate education at Rice.

Don't get me wrong—I was still an integrationist, more than ever. In high school (against the wishes of my English teacher), I had read *Black Like Me*, Texan author John Howard Griffin's account of how he had dyed his white skin a deep brown in order to experience segregation from the other side of the color line. Reading his powerful testament, I seethed against the stupidity and injustice of racism. I had listened intently on my portable radio the previous summer, in June of 1964, as the successful Senate cloture vote assured the passage of the Civil Rights Bill submitted by the now-slain President Kennedy and pushed through a reluctant Congress by my new larger-than-life Texas hero, Lyndon B. Johnson. It had been an exhilarating moment, and one that made me believe that "history" and "progress" were firmly intertwined.

I was enormously proud that Rice University had gone to court in the early 1960s in order to "break the will" of its benefactor, the early Texas cotton exporter William Marsh Rice, who had left his fortune for the higher education of "white" Texans. The university won the suit and planned to admit its first black undergraduates in my sophomore year.

And yet those alarm bells kept ringing when I found myself actually "integrating"! All I could think about was the fact that the people sitting and talking in my dorm room were black—

this took irrational precedence in my mind over anything they were saying to me—and I was on pins and needles until they left. It took years of experience and introspection, of reading and thinking, of long talks with my professors and ultimately with my own black and white students and colleagues, before I was able to jettison most of that unwanted psychological baggage left in place by the ingrained racial norms of my upbringing.

What was happening in that swimming pool, in that dormitory room? What had I been thinking about, and *not* thinking about? Some clues, perhaps, can be found in my tattered seventh-grade copy of *Texas History Movies* and in a photograph etched in my memory, which was taken of me when I was six years old. The photograph showed three children standing with their backs against a whitewashed wall. There were fruit jars filled with preserves on the shelf above our heads. We were in the cool cement basement of my cousin Charlie's farmhouse, escaping the blistering Texas summer. Charlie, about five years old, stood in the middle, beating the heat by wearing nothing but his underwear, his bare belly protruding toward the camera. I was the skinny one on the left, in a not-so-slick cowboy outfit: western shirt, western belt (*and* suspenders—I truly was a skinny kid). I was also wearing a weirdly silly grin, my eyes averted to my right. Who was standing to our left? My answer would depend on when you asked me.

When my mother handed me a copy of this picture a little more than a decade ago, almost forty years after the photograph was taken, I saw a neatly dressed black girl, slightly older than Charlie and me, looking deeply embarrassed. But this was not what I saw when I looked at this image, over and over again, as I was growing up in Henrietta.

What my mother showed me was a print made from a slide—both, alas, now lost, and my mom no longer living. But I remember the image all too well. The slide was what came to be known in my family as "The Comedy." For years, every time people gathered at our house to see slides of the latest family reunion or vacation, my sister and I would demand, whatever the intended subject of the evening's entertainment, to see the "comedy" first. Every time. I suppose that a dorky little cowboy wannabe and his half-dressed cousin are funny enough in themselves, but that is really not what we were laughing at.

We were laughing at Gwendolyn, the daughter of my uncle Clyde's tenant farmers. We were laughing at the feigned suggestion of "integration" (and also perhaps at the faint hint of intimacy) because *not* to laugh would have meant taking the photograph, and the person depicted there, seriously. Not taking blacks seriously as individuals—and at the same time reacting to their incongruous presence with hysteria (either comedic or tragic)—was a major part of our "way of life."

I know Gwendolyn's name today only because Charlie can tell me. I don't remember meeting her, nor posing with her in the cellar. She existed for me only in that picture, which became a kind of twisted icon—but an icon representing what? She was—and it pains me deeply to say this today—just a "nigger" for us. This is how we had learned to look at the black people around us, past and present. The following cartoons show what we learned in the seventh grade about slavery in prerevolutionary Texas.

I'm sure that my classmates and I found these images funny as hell, but I doubt that we noticed the obvious contradictions

between the text and the captions. Coach Brockman certainly did not point out to us the ironic fact that the progressive Mexican state laws described here by Patton and Rosenfield were unenforced and completely disregarded by the Anglo-American slaveholders whom Stephen F. Austin led into Texas as "colonists" in the 1820s. And in the nine pages that follow these scenes in *Texas History Movies*—a section recounting in fond detail the adventures of the famous Jim Bowie—there is not a hint amid the duels and Indian fights as to Bowie's lucrative Louisiana slave-smuggling ring (in partnership with the pirate Jean Lafitte).

The only black person identified by name in my copy of *Texas History Movies* was Richmond, the slave who accompanied Stephen's father Moses Austin upon his fateful departure in 1820 from Missouri to San Antonio—a quest that legally opened Texas to Anglo-American settlement. The following cartoon shows my picture of Richmond.

It was hard to know how to relate to the "Negro" next to you in the swimming pool or the dorm room, given the cumulative power of the images of "niggers" that surrounded us in virtually every popular medium. Even black-faced minstrel shows were not dead in the Henrietta of the 1950s. I watched my dad perform in one held for charity in the old high school auditorium, wondering even as a child what must have been going through the minds of the black families that I could turn around and see behind me, watching the show from the balconies. As a teenager, I even took part in the black-faced comedic ritual myself before an all-white Baptist church group, at the behest of our Mississippi-born youth minister. It is difficult to describe adequately the mix of fear and shame I felt when, on the way home from

(COPYRIGHT: TEXAS STATE HISTORICAL ASSOCIATION, AUSTIN, TEXAS.)

the church and still wearing shoe polish and outlandish clothes, I found myself next to a "carload" of genuine African Americans as I pulled into Billy Womack's Texaco station. I didn't stay to get gas that night.

It was at Rice University that I at last found the analytical tools and the intellectual freedom, as well as the new social experiences, that enabled me to take a long, hard look at myself and my culture. I didn't find all the answers in my four years there, but I at least began to ask some of the right questions.

My facile certainty as a Rice freshman that I and my country were on the fast track to a progressive and cosmopolitan future was shaken to the core by the events of the mid-1960s. I wept with pride and empathy when I listened to Lyndon Johnson's "We Shall Overcome" speech to Congress on March 15, 1965; I exulted in his signing of the Voting Rights Act on August 6; and then felt shock and despair when the Watts Riot blazed through Los Angeles less than a week later, a harbinger of flames still to come.

The Vietnam conflict was also heating up, and I was at first a strong supporter of President Johnson's policies. It was "racist," I argued to my antiwar classmates, to defend freedom in West Berlin but not in South Vietnam. But as the war brought more and more tales of senseless destruction, the fight seemed destined to produce tragedy rather than triumph. How could the "American story" go so wrong? Could history (which I had associated uncritically with progress) start running backward?

I had come to the university with a vague intention of majoring in history. The events of the tumultuous 1960s cemented my decision. I wanted to know what made Americans, and especially Southerners, think and act the way they did. I wanted to know if Americans were different from other people and, if so, how and why. I wanted to know where bigotry came from. I wanted desperately, in other words, to know more about myself and my troubled nation, and I looked to history for answers.

It was outside the classroom, however, that I began to fully realize the complexity of Texas's racial hierarchy. On the Rice campus we were surrounded by Gnomes, pronounced "guh-no-mees" by the students who had given them the name. They were our janitors and our gardeners, and they were almost all "Mexicans" (or as our student newspaper put it jocularly, "Hispano-Aztecs"). There were extremely few Hispanics among my classmates—they were almost as rare in the student population as non-Mexicans were among the Gnomes. And yet they *were* there, and had been present in tiny numbers for years, in a student body that had been theoretically limited to "whites" by the last will and testament of William Marsh Rice. Having grown up in a society that seemed to make a very important distinction between "whites" and "Mexicans," I was both confused and intrigued.

As I came to realize how little I actually knew about the Mexican dimension of Texas's past and present, that tricolor banner from among the six flags began to interest me. As my first history honors project I chose an analysis of Mexican immigration policies during the early years of Anglo-American settlement in Texas. Why, I wondered, had the Mexicans been foolish enough to actually *encourage* all those dangerous and probably prejudiced Anglos to follow Moses and Stephen Austin across the Sabine River? And what had made those Anglo settlers so willing to become Mexican citizens? Was it possible that Anglos and Mexicans had once actually *liked* each other?

It was through the purest coincidence that in that same spring semester I met and began dating Lynn Perez, a student at the University of Houston, and my future wife. Lynn's mother had been a Hoosier, but after her untimely death in the mid-1950s Lynn and her four siblings were raised in Houston by their bilingual father, Raul Perez. His family had fled the Mexican Revolution of 1910–1917 not long after he was born in Piedras Negras, a border town on the "other" side of the Río Grande. My gradual introduction to Mexican Texas began in 1966, and I'm still learning.

My work as a student of history, however, was taking me in a different direction. In my courses in the history of the South I came to read virtually everything published by a Southern historian at Yale University, C. Vann Woodward. *The Strange Career of Jim Crow*, Woodward's study of the origins of segregation, particularly gripped me, for it argued that segregation in Southern society was neither foreordained nor natural. It was *made*—painstakingly constructed in those post-Reconstruction years about which *Texas History Movies* (and most of my textbooks) had so little to say. To me, Woodward's book showed that the world that produced the Fred Douglass School on Henrietta's edge was not the only possible world, and that the kind of rigid segregation it represented did not have the ancient and respectable pedigree claimed for it by Governor Faubus and its other defenders.

It was a liberating message, but a double-edged one. It meant that history really could go backward if an institution as perverse as segregation could follow in the wake of the promises of the First Reconstruction—even the promises of equal treatment under the law that had been written into the United States Constitution as the Fourteenth and Fifteenth Amendments. Could the same fate await the foundations of the "Second Reconstruction," the Civil Rights Act and the Voting Rights Act, now only a few years old?

When the time came to apply to graduate schools, Yale was at the top of my list, simply because C. Vann Woodward was teaching there. When Yale said "yes," I didn't hesitate. In the late summer of 1968, Lynn and I hitched a U-Haul trailer to my Buick Skylark and left on the day after our Houston wedding for faraway New Haven, Connecticut.

But I had not really left Texas behind. My first course with Woodward at Yale was a seminar on American race relations. I chose as my term paper topic the changing status of the Tejanos (the Texans of Mexican origin) during the years in which the Anglo strangers in their land became the majority. What, I also wanted to know, had been the Tejanos' role in the Texas Revolution of 1835–1836? How did they fare in the Texas Republic, which maintained its independence for the next decade? What could their fate tell us about the racial views of the Anglos? How did the hierarchy of race begin? Had there been ethnic hostility from the start?

Through the next three years of graduate school, the seminar paper written for C. Vann Woodward turned into my doctoral dissertation, written under the direction of Yale's historian of the American West, Howard R. Lamar. As I researched the "strange career" of anti-Mexican prejudice and discrimination in early

Texas, I found that supposedly immutable hatreds and hierarchies had a less venerable origin than I had been taught. In short, by the time that I earned my degree from Yale and began teaching at North Carolina State University, I had come to doubt the widespread opinion that the Texas Revolution had been the inevitable fruit of the "age old prejudice of race" (as displayed in the first cartoon below from *Texas History Movies*).

These three cartoons—stressing the racial, political, and cultural gap between Anglos and Mexicans—represented the dominant conventional wisdom in the twentieth century. The preeminent Texas historian Eugene C. Barker wrote in 1911 that "at bottom the Texas Revolution was the product of the racial and political inheritances of the two peoples." Over the years, Barker and his academic adherents gradually softened what at first appeared to be a crude theory of racial determinism by emphasizing instead a "culture conflict" between Anglo and Mexican that made the revolution inevitable. But the basic interpretation of ethnic cleavage as the essential cause remained intact. And it cast a long shadow. As late as 1991, historian Paul D. Lack argued

(Copyright: Texas State Historical Association, Austin, Texas.)

that "the focus on culture conflict has remained the starting point for all explanations of the background of the Texas Revolution and has been emphasized by recent scholars." But Lack acknowledged that my Yale dissertation had challenged the prevailing view when I maintained

> that racial conflict bore little responsibility for the origins of the Texas Revolution. . . . Crisp argued [said Lack, that] emigrants to Texas in the 1820s and 1830s came without a full-blown set of negative preconceptions to serve as a taproot for rebellion and learned to get along reasonably well with the Tejano elite. [Crisp] concluded that the ugliest expression of racism triumphed with and after the Texas Revolution, its ironic consequence rather than its cause.

As I labored to turn the dissertation into a book, I found myself in agreement with John H. Jenkins, who published the ten-volume *Papers of the Texas Revolution* in 1973. Poring through the thousands of documents Jenkins had compiled, I understood his blunt assessment that very little that had been published on the revolution could be trusted. All too often, "facts" about this conflict proved to be unsubstantiated by the evidence. Assertions regarding "what really happened" turned out to be myth. I was also beginning to suspect that many historians had projected onto the past their assumptions about racial antagonism in the present.

By the late 1980s, I felt that I was developing an unassailable case for my thesis that ethnic cleavage had been more a consequence than a motivating cause of the Texas Revolution. I knew that during the sesquicentennial decade of the Texas Republic (1986–1996), there would be a horde of historical taxidermists at work, doing their best to portray that interesting little nation in the most flattering of poses. I hoped that the republic would also become the object of study of a few historical pathologists, who would strive not merely to identify and to curse the crippling infection of racism, but also to understand the conditions that fostered its growth.

Toward the end of 1992, I was completing an article laying out my revisionist case that the Texas Revolution was less a product of ethnic friction than a precipitating cause of it. But only a few weeks after sending my final corrections to the publisher, I found myself reading with dismay a manifestly racist speech by Sam Houston, the idol of my Texas boyhood. The speech, quoted in a prize-winning new book by Paul D. Lack, shocked me because it upset not only my best understanding of what the Texas Revolution meant but also my plans to publish a book about what I thought I knew.

Over the course of the past decade, my search for what Houston and others actually said and did has propelled me along a twisted path through some of the fondest myths of the Texas Revolution. This little book is the story of one historian's attempt to separate Texas myth from Texas history. Along the way, I've been forced to tackle more than one Texas mystery. The tale begins with Sam Houston riding toward the small South Texas settlement of Refugio—where he would be forced to make that speech.

· One ·

SAM HOUSTON'S
SPEECHWRITERS

As HE APPROACHED THE ENCAMPMENT OF VOLUNTEER SOL-
diers near Refugio in January of 1836, General Sam Houston
knew that the revolt against Mexico was spinning out of control.
He was near the southern tip of Texas, many miles from where
he believed that he and his rebel army ought to be. Despite its
name, Houston knew that this isolated spot would provide no
refuge for his men in the spring, when Mexican armies would be
marching northward across the Río Grande.

The Texan soldiers, however, were dreaming of crossing that
river in the other direction, just as soon as enough horses could
be rounded up for them. On the other side lay Matamoros, and
the poorly provisioned Texan troops lusted after the bounty reputedly awaiting them in that Mexican port city. Houston
thought that an offensive expedition against Matamoros—which
would have to cross another 150 miles of unpopulated prairies
before reaching the Río Grande—would be madness. But because the men camped near Refugio were volunteers, the Major

General of the Texan army had no authority to give them orders. Houston was going to have to rely on persuasion.

The adobe houses surrounding the old Spanish mission of Nuestra Señora del Refugio (Our Lady of Refuge) reminded Houston that he was deep in Hispanic Texas, where few settlers from the United States had penetrated. The English that was heard in the town of Refugio often carried a Gaelic lilt, betraying the origins of many recently arrived Irish Catholic immigrants who now attended services at the mission church with their Mexican neighbors. The Irish were carving out farms and ranches from generous land grants given them by a Mexican government belatedly trying to dilute the American influence in its vulnerable northeastern province of Texas.

It was a futile effort. Anglo-Americans continued to pour in, even during the years from 1830 to 1834, when immigration from the United States was officially banned. Some of the Americans who came during those years simply ignored the Mexican law. Others, like Houston himself, used legal loopholes opened by the influential *empresario* (or colonization agent) Stephen F. Austin. Houston first splashed across the Red River into Texas from Indian country (today's Oklahoma) on December 2, 1832; by Christmas, he had secured a land grant of over four thousand acres in Austin's colony.

When he entered Texas, Houston carried with him an American passport identifying him as an official United States peace envoy to the nomadic Comanche Indians. But this was in all probability merely a convenient "cover" for a mission of far greater significance to both Houston and his close friend and confidante, President Andrew Jackson. Though Jackson's earlier heavy-handed efforts to obtain Texas from Mexico through diplomatic pressure had been unsuccessful, the president was a persistent and resourceful chief executive. No doubt he was pleased that someone he trusted would be on the scene in Texas.

As for Houston himself, the immense province presented great opportunities for reviving a political career that had ended disastrously in 1829 when a failed marriage led him to abandon the governorship of Tennessee and—to the consternation of his political allies—retreat to live with the Cherokee Indians. He sought out the same band who had once adopted him as a runaway teenager and given him the name *Co-lo-neh*, the Raven. During his second self-imposed exile from "white society" Houston spent months in despondency, and earned a new Cherokee name: *Oo-tse-tee Ar-dee-tah-skee*, Big Drunk. But the prospects of a Texan adventure gave Houston a new lease on life.

After less than three months in Texas, Houston was elected in February 1833 as a delegate to a convention that was expected to demand separate statehood for Texas within the Republic of Mexico. A large and sparsely peopled frontier region when Mexico gained independence from Spain in 1821, Texas had been grafted onto the more heavily populated province of Coahuila in 1824 to create the unwieldy joint state of *Coahuila y Tejas* (Coahuila and Texas) until the population of Texas could justify its separation.

Houston anticipated a more drastic kind of separation, however. Soon after his arrival, he had concluded that most American settlers in Texas favored eventual annexation by the United States. Even then, he knew that a determined minority were prepared to use violence to hasten that day.

Between his election to the 1833 convention and its first meeting in April, Houston crossed the international boundary into Louisiana to post an important letter to President Jackson. After extensive travel across Texas, Houston reported that he was sure that "nineteen-twentieths of the population of the province" desired "the acquisition of Texas by the United States." He was certain that the upcoming convention would demand at least the splitting of Coahuila and Texas, and predicted that "unless Mexico is soon restored to order" Texas would take action to separate itself completely from the Mexican nation.

Houston was ready for any contingency. "I may make Texas my abiding place!" he told Jackson, vowing that "in adopting this course, I will *never forget* the country of my birth." He promised to keep Jackson well informed of "any facts, which could enable you, during your administration, to acquire Texas."

The Texan convention of 1833 selected not the newcomer Houston, but Stephen F. Austin to carry to Mexico City its demand that Texas become a state separate from Coahuila. As the *empresario* who had first led Americans into Texas as legal colonists in the 1820s, Austin remained their unofficial leader. His motto had always been "Fidelity to Mexico." But his plea for separate statehood received no support from Mexican officials in the national capital.

Discouraged, Austin incautiously wrote a letter to political leaders in San Antonio de Béxar urging these Tejanos to start organizing Texas into a separate Mexican state without waiting for permission from the central government. When word of this letter leaked out, Austin was accused of treason, arrested on his way home, and jailed in Mexico City for more than a year. By the time he finally made his way back to Texas in the fall of 1835, both the political situation and Austin's attitude had changed drastically. Mexico was engulfed in civil war, and Austin was convinced that war was also the only recourse for Texas.

An armed struggle had finally come, but not in the fashion that Houston and most proponents of the American annexation of Texas had anticipated. Fighting had erupted in 1835 far to the south of Texas in the Mexican interior, where rival "Centralist" and "Federalist" factions clashed over the best form of government for Mexico. The Centralists wanted a stronger national government, unchecked by the state governments, which had been awarded considerable power by the Mexican Federal Constitution of 1824.

Conversely, the supporters of Federalism (which included the great majority of Anglo-American settlers in Texas) defended "states' rights" in Mexico—including the rights of the states to determine who could bear arms, who could immigrate into the country, and, for at least some Federalists, even whether their citizens could continue to hold African American slaves in bondage. Clearly, separate statehood under a Federalist constitution would give the recently arrived emigrants from the United States far more control over their own affairs.

In Mexico City, the mercurial President Antonio López de Santa Anna had turned against the Federalist allies who put him in office in 1833 and come out strongly for Centralism. When the states of Zacatecas and Coahuila y Tejas challenged Santa Anna's right to disarm their militias and disband their legislatures, he imposed his will with brute force. He crushed the revolts in Zacatecas and Coahuila, and sent a few hundred troops to reinforce the Mexican garrison in San Antonio de Béxar, the largest Texas municipality. The Texans were ordered to turn over to the military authorities the leading opponents of the Centralist regime, as well as all unauthorized weapons. This demand was summarily refused, and soon the Mexican troops in San Antonio found themselves besieged by a coalition of rebellious Tejanos, Anglo-Texan colonists, a few Federalists from south of the Río Grande—and scores of volunteers from the United States who had rushed to Texas at the first sign of a revolt against Mexico.

But was it really a revolt against Mexico? Stephen Austin and Sam Houston each believed that secession from that nation was both the war's most likely outcome and, for them, its most desirable ultimate goal. However, to admit that objective openly would alienate the Mexican Federalists who were helping in the fight against Santa Anna. It would in effect unite all of Mexico (with a population of eight million) against the Texan rebels, whose fighting force could not exceed a few thousand men. (The total population of Texas, excluding Indians, was less than 40,000.) Both Austin and Houston saw the advantage in proceeding cautiously.

This conservative position was adopted by the Texan convention (known as the "Consultation"), which met in the fall of 1835. To secure the support of Mexican Federalists, the Consultation voted (33 to 14) to embrace the principles of the Mexican Constitution of 1824, although it reserved the right of secession if "constitutional" rule could not be restored in the Mexican nation. The delegates to the Consultation also appointed a Provisional Governor and a General Council to oversee Texas and direct the revolt. Though it was not immediately obvious, this governmental scheme was a formula for disaster. Most of the members of the new General Council had supported the declaration aligning the rebellious Texans with the Mexican Federalists. On the other hand, the man appointed as governor, Henry Smith, was a firebrand who had refused to vote for anything short of Texan independence.

In the meantime, the Texan rebels besieging San Antonio finally took that city (also known simply as Béxar) in early December, fighting as Federalists under a Mexican tricolor with "1824" inscribed on the central white stripe. They compelled the Centralist forces under General Martín Perfecto de Cos to surrender both the city and the adjacent fortified mission known as the Alamo. Cos and his men were released on the condition that they leave Texas and never again take up arms against the Federalist Constitution of 1824. With Cos gone, Texas was free of Centralist troops, but this success brought about a difficult question: what next?

The first answer came from the strategically important fortress (or *presidio*) at Goliad, about ninety miles down the San Antonio River below Béxar. Cos had left this post lightly defended as he marched into Texas from the seacoast earlier in 1835, and the presidio had fallen easily to the rebels in October. On December 20, the volunteer soldiers quartered there signed the "Goliad Declaration of Independence," which proclaimed Texas a "free, sovereign, and independent State." This declaration was suppressed by the General Council, which deemed it premature at best.

The Goliad Declaration of Independence was also fiercely opposed by Dr. James Grant, a charismatic Scotsman with large landholdings south of the Río Grande. Grant had been among the leaders of the Federalist forces in Coahuila before the arrival of Santa Anna's troops forced him to flee to Texas. Although he held no formal command, Grant was the leading spirit among a large group of volunteer soldiers who marched out of San Antonio in late December, determined to continue on the offensive by advancing into the Mexican state of Tamaulipas and capturing the important city of Matamoros. Grant was convinced that a Texan force crossing the Río Grande would be joined by enthusiastic Mexican Federalists.

Governor Henry Smith had originally entrusted the prospective Matamoros expedition to Sam Houston, but Houston already had his hands full. He had been named the commanding Major General of the regular Texan army by the Consultation. This was a fine-sounding title, but the army had attracted almost no recruits, and the volunteers already in the field had not been placed under his command. Faced with the formidable task of creating an army from scratch, Houston handed the responsibility for the Matamoros expedition over to James Bowie, the famous Louisiana knife-fighter who had settled in Texas and married into a prominent Mexican family in San Antonio. Houston's orders, written in mid-December, made it clear that Bowie was free to drop the idea of a Matamoros expedition if he thought that it could not be successful or if insufficient resources were available.

Houston was rapidly coming to the conclusion that an attack across the Río Grande was a very bad idea. In fact, he was beginning to have doubts about the feasibility of defeating the Mexican army even in southwestern Texas. In January, he ordered

Bowie to San Antonio, where Houston had already directed that the fortifications in that city be demolished. The Texan commander thought that the Alamo should also be blown up and abandoned, and its artillery removed eastward.

Houston hoped that both Bowie and Governor Smith would agree with him that the Texans should not try to hold onto frontier fortresses, but should instead be prepared to fall back across the rivers of central Texas. Most likely, Houston contemplated luring Santa Anna's invading forces deep into East Texas, where they would be in unfamiliar and unfriendly territory far from their base of operations and vulnerable to attack by more "volunteers" (or perhaps even United States troops) arriving from across the border. Governor Smith, however, refused to authorize the abandonment of the Alamo, and Bowie, who believed that the enemy could be stopped in the West, set about strengthening the poorly equipped "fort."

At least Bowie agreed with Houston that an expedition to Matamoros was ill-advised. James Grant, however, having already marched out of San Antonio with most of that post's men and supplies, was still eager to proceed. His forces reached Goliad in early January. There, he angrily demanded that the flag of independence raised on December 20 be pulled down, so that its message would not alienate Mexican Federalists in the interior. Tensions were running high at Goliad, but no more so than at the provisional Texan capital of San Felipe de Austin, where Governor Smith and the General Council were completely at loggerheads over the conduct of the rebellion.

The Council, which very much favored the capture of Matamoros and cooperation with supposed Mexican Federalist forces in the interior, had authorized Dr. Grant's close associate Frank W. Johnson to command such an expedition, despite Governor Smith's earlier orders placing Houston in control. When Johnson hesitated before accepting the offer, the Council gave the Matamoros expedition to a young Texan officer (and West Point dropout) by the name of James W. Fannin. But when Johnson changed his mind and claimed the command after all, the Council revoked neither man's commission. Now the ill-fated Matamoros expedition had two commanders in addition to Houston—actually three, if one counts the headstrong Dr. Grant, who seemed to be taking orders from no one.

Matters in the provisional capital proceeded from bad to worse. Governor Smith had vetoed Fannin's appointment, but the General Council overruled him, furious at his imperious ways. The Council then impeached Smith for good measure. He refused to give up his office and attempted instead to disband the Council. Neither side was willing to back down, and soon there was no effective government in San Felipe. Yet Fannin, Johnson, and Grant were all preparing to carry their war beyond the boundaries of this completely dysfunctional "provisional state" of Texas.

The various commanders went their own ways. Fannin set out eastward to recruit more troops for the expedition, while Johnson and Grant hurriedly marched from Goliad in the direction of the Río Grande, allowing most of their men to pause near Refugio while they and their wranglers crossed the Nueces River (the border between Texas and Tamaulipas) to round up the hundreds of horses needed for the intended descent on Matamoros.

A Matamoros expedition might have made good military sense early in the conflict, because the exiled Mexican Federalist General José Antonio Mexía planned to cooperate with the Texans by leading an amphibious assault from New Orleans against Tampico, another port city on the northeastern coast of Mexico. However, Mexía's attempt to take this city in mid-November ended in a debacle, with Mexía in flight and many of his volunteers from the United States captured and executed in Tampico for piracy.

This was the situation—spinning rapidly out of control—faced by Sam Houston, the general with virtually no army at his command, as he approached Refugio in the middle of January 1836. Houston was by now desperate to stop what he saw as a suicidal strategy that would divide the soon-to-be outnumbered Texan forces and send the best troops headlong into unfamiliar (and probably unfriendly) territory against the advancing Mexican army. It was a strategy quite the opposite of his own design for victory.

Unable to assert legal authority over the predominantly volunteer troops, who insisted on electing their own leaders and determining their own course of action, Houston would have to turn politician and rely on his skills of persuasion. Appearing unexpectedly in the Texan camp, he told the gathered soldiers that he did not share Dr. Grant's faith that Mexican Federalist allies were waiting to join them in Matamoros. Earlier in the day, Houston had written to Governor Smith that he was going to attempt to dissuade the rank and file from acting on Grant's "hope or belief that the Mexicans will cooperate with us. I have no confidence in them," wrote Houston, "and the disaster at Tampico should teach us a lesson to be noted in our future operations."

But Houston's distrust was apparently not limited to the Mexicans south of the Nueces and the Río Grande. His address to the soldiers at Refugio seemed to exhibit quite openly Houston's own racial prejudices. The words of the speech were harsh. They accused the Tejanos, the Mexicans living in Texas, of aiding the enemy in great numbers. Houston denounced as even more dangerous those Texas Mexicans who had retired to their farms and ranches "apparently to idly observe the war." "He who is not with us," he warned, "is against us."

The speech grounded the argument for the independence of Texas from Mexico in the concept of fundamental and immutable differences between Americans and Mexicans:

> Since it is impossible to call forth any sympathy from our fellow Mexican citizens and no support is to be expected from this side and as they let us, the smallest of all the provinces, struggle without any aid, let us then, comrades, sever that link that binds us to that rusty chain of the Mexican Confederation; let us break off the live slab from the dying cactus that it may not dry up with the remainder; let us plant it anew that it may spring luxuriantly out of the fruitful savannah. Nor will the vigor of the descendants of the sturdy north ever mix with the phlegm of the indolent Mexicans, no matter how long we may live among them. Two different tribes on the same hunting ground will never get along together. The tomahawk will ever fly and the scalping knife will never rest until the last of either one tribe or the other is either destroyed or is a slave. And I ask, comrades, will we ever bend our necks as slaves, ever quietly watch the destruction of our property and the annihilation of our guaranteed rights? No! Never! Too well I know my people. The last drop of our blood would flow before we would bow under the yoke of these half-Indians.

Houston's oratorical effort was only partially successful. Most of his listeners continued to favor an expedition to Matamoros, but they agreed to wait for Fannin, who was due to return soon with the recruits and the supplies that could make their adventure a success.

Houston's speech had a far greater impact on me than on the soldiers at Refugio. I remember distinctly that, upon reviewing it in its entirety in December 1992, I was stunned and disbelieving. The words seemed so unlike Houston. Part of my reaction, I suppose, could be attributed to nostalgia for my childhood image of Sam Houston, the adopted Cherokee. Given his long and friendly relationships with Native Americans, how could Houston revile Mexicans by calling them "half-Indians"? But more than nostalgia was involved.

The speech contradicted much of what I thought that I had learned in more than two decades of investigating the causes and consequences of the Texas Revolution. Yet here it was before me in black and white: Houston's bitterly racist, anti-Mexican speech was duly listed as document #1791 in the fourth volume of John Jenkins's *Papers of the Texas Revolution*. Had Eugene C. Barker been right all along when he said that "at bottom the Texas Revolution was the product of the racial and political inheritances of the two peoples"?

I knew that this had been the prevailing view of the conflict since the mid-nineteenth century, when it was argued that Mexicans were so inherently incapable of self-government that the Anglo-Texans who suffered under Mexican rule had no choice but to revolt against their corrupt and tyrannical governors. This sensibility certainly informed Mrs. Anna J. Hardwicke Penny-backer's *New History of Texas*, a staple in the public schools of the state for forty years after its publication in 1888. Here is how she described the relationship between Anglos and Mexicans after the passage of the law of 1830 forbidding further American immigration:

> Other nations were heartily welcomed, but for the United States, whose inhabitants had changed Texas from a wilderness into a civilized State, Mexico had nothing but fear and hatred. . . . Mexico being constantly in the throes of revolutions, was conscious of her own weakness; she feared if the Americans continued to settle in Texas, they might rebel, and with the help of their country, throw off the Mexican yoke. Hence she resolved to keep out other Americans, and to crush the spirit of those who were already within her boundaries. Looking at the matter as one may, no humane person can find justice in Mexico's rule of Texas. That she was vastly mistaken in the nature of the men she wished to crush is shown by the events of the next few years.

Early twentieth-century scholars of the Texas Revolution, following Barker's lead, couched the clash between peoples in the more sophisticated terms of "culture conflict" and "differences in folkways." But through the 1950s the basic implication of their interpretations remained the same as before: the Texas Revolution was the result of fundamental differences between the Anglo and Hispanic peoples—and the Anglos did not suffer in the comparison.

However, by the late 1960s and early 1970s historical scholarship, like the society in which it was embedded, was changing dramatically. The result was essentially to turn the traditional explanation for the Texas Revolution on its head. Instead of laying the responsibility for the revolt at the feet of Mexican deficiencies (either racial or cultural), a new and radicalized generation of historians saw the origins of the conflict in the prejudices of Anglo-American bigots. Accusations of *racism*, in other words, refuted and largely replaced traditional interpretations that had revolved around notions of inherent differences between racial and ethnic groups. But while racism was no doubt a more defensible causal explanation than the doctrine of race, it seemed to me nearly as simplistic as the old, discredited rationale. The identity of the villains was reversed, but the "age-old" racial dichotomy between the conflicting sides remained intact.

The reasons for my dissatisfaction with both race and racism as candidates for the primary cause of the Texas Revolution were in part philosophical. As I studied in depth the relationships between Anglos and Mexicans in Texas, I proceeded with the belief that neither imputed racial differences nor the racist attitudes that insisted upon their validity should be taken as immutable "givens" in any historical situation.

There were also empirical reasons for my discontent. Neither the "racial" nor the "racist" hypothesis matched the evidence that was piling up as I burrowed more deeply into the documentary records of the Texas Revolution and the Texas Republic. Early relations between Anglo newcomers and the Mexicans they encountered in Texas, while complex, appeared more often cordial than hostile. It seemed to me that conflict between the two groups was not so much an immediate *cause* as it was an eventual *consequence* of Texas's separation from Mexico.

The fighting began not over culturally sensitive questions of language, religion, race, or slavery, but rather over issues that divided so many other frontier areas of Mexico from the central government: disagreements over states' rights and local autonomy; exorbitant tariffs and the haphazard suppression of smuggling; inefficient and arbitrary administration of the laws; and the weakness and corruption of the army. Even in areas of Mexico where Anglo-American settlement was sparse or nonexistent—in California, New Mexico, and Yucatán, for example—there developed widespread separatist sentiment, a willingness to welcome American immigrants even against the wishes of Mexico City, and an opposition to Centralism that sparked violent revolts against the national government in the mid-1830s.

The Texan struggle, born ironically in the midst of a Mexican civil war, was portrayed by its earliest leaders as the "last rallying point of liberty" for the "republicans of Mexico"—as part of "the great work of laying the cornerstone of liberty in the great Mexican republic." Such sentiments became harder to maintain, however, as the rebels found the success of their cause more dependent on the aid of American volunteers than of Mexican Federalists. Even as the General Council of the provisional revolutionary government of Texas was endorsing cooperation with "any Mexican Liberal, whose cause is our cause, as opposed to military despotism," an aggressive minority of pro-independence men within the government were trying to redefine the issue. "The Mexican people and the Anglo-Americans in Texas," they insisted, "never can be one and the same people. A civil compact can never bind together long [sic] people who differ so widely in their pursuits, their religion, their Languages and their ideas of civil liberty."

In the same vein, Governor Henry Smith was increasingly reluctant to cooperate with Mexicans of any political stripe. He even opposed allowing Tejanos to vote for delegates to the Convention of March 1836, which declared Texas to be free of Mexico. But Smith's veto of the bill calling for the Convention was overruled by the General Council, and on March 2 three native Mexican delegates became signers of the Texas Declaration of Independence. One of these delegates, an ardent Federalist from Yucatán by the name of Lorenzo de Zavala, was selected by the Convention to be the first vice president of the new Republic of Texas.

This level of *mexicano* participation, even as separation from Mexico became an avowed goal of the struggle, is powerful evidence in itself that the Texan revolt was a much more complex event than a "race war." Yet the consequences of a war for complete separation from Mexico were profound. The Revolution radically restructured political and ethnic alignments, accelerated and redirected economic and population growth, and created an environment of danger and uncertainty in which racism has historically flourished.

The shifting dynamics of cooperation and confrontation between "Mexicans" and "Americans" in Texas are most clearly reflected in the career of one of the first Texans to take up arms (in April 1835) against what he called the "aggressions" of "the tyrannical government of Santa Anna." This Texan—for the moment, he will remain anonymous—was a family friend of Stephen F. Austin and an ambitious businessman and rancher. At the age of twenty-nine, he led a scouting and ranging company for Austin's "Army of the People" as it drove General Cos and his forces from San Antonio in December 1835. And the following February, when fortunes turned, this Texan warrior found himself in the Alamo (along with James Bowie and almost two hundred other rebels), surrounded by the forces that General Santa Anna had marched to Texas through the Mexican winter.

Because he knew Spanish, the Texan officer was chosen to slip out through the Mexican lines at night in order to seek reinforcements. But by the time he returned with a few dozen armed riders, it was too late. The Alamo had fallen, and every defender inside had been killed. Turning eastward, he and his mounted men joined the retreating Sam Houston, and then fought fiercely against the Mexican army when Houston turned the tables on Santa Anna and captured him at the Battle of San Jacinto less than seven weeks after the Alamo's fall. (We will return to the battles of the Alamo and San Jacinto in later chapters.)

Following the successful revolt against Mexico, the new president of the Lone Star Republic, Sam Houston, confirmed this energetic cavalryman (now a lieutenant colonel) as commandant of the dangerous frontier post at San Antonio, telling him, "You know the enemy whom you have to guard against—therefore I rely upon your ability, patriotism, and watchfulness . . . " It was in his capacity as commandant at Béxar that this patriot gave the official eulogy during the burial of the ashes of the slain Alamo defenders when they were finally laid to rest in 1837. The following year, he resigned his army commission to serve a three-year term as a senator in the Congress of the Republic of Texas. During his second and third years in office, he served as chairman of the important Senate Committee on Military Affairs. After leaving Congress, the retired officer and senator was twice elected mayor of San Antonio, in 1841 and 1842.

Given this list of accomplishments, it may come as a surprise for some to learn that all of this dashing Texan's speeches in Congress, all of his letters to his friend and political ally Sam Houston—even his funeral oration over the Alamo ashes—were written or spoken in Spanish! For their author, a fifth-generation citizen of San Antonio by the name of Juan Nepomuceno Seguín, did not speak or write English.

The trajectory of Juan Seguín's life during and after the Texas Revolution should cast doubt on the adequacy of Anglo racism as the core explanation of the cause and the course of the conflict. His career is hardly what one would expect of a Mexican in Texas following a revolution that was essentially a "race war"! Nevertheless, signs of racial and ethnic cleavage were visible during and after the revolt. And, eventually, racial antagonisms within the Texas Republic would entangle even Juan Seguín.

Some of the most serious interethnic conflict came in the immediate aftermath of Houston's victory at San Jacinto. Thousands of new American volunteers swelled the ranks of the Texan army at a time that there was nothing much for them to do and, perhaps appropriately, nothing much to pay them with. Not surprisingly, this kind of army turned nasty and insubordinate, resisting discipline and more than once coming close to overthrowing the civilian Texan government. (Houston himself had been severely wounded at San Jacinto and left Texas shortly thereafter to seek medical attention in New Orleans.)

When the bulk of the army was garrisoned at Victoria, near the southwestern frontier, life in this once predominantly Mexican town was severely disrupted. Even Tejanos who had actively supported the Revolution were subjected to assaults and assassination attempts. Most of the original citizens were forced to flee. When Anglo squatters moved in to claim the spoils, Victoria's Irish Catholic mayor, John J. Linn (one of the few citizens of Hispanic Victoria to stay on after the army's arrival), accused these "remorseless" newcomers of espousing a creed of "total extermination of the Mexican race and the appropriation of their property to the individual use of the exterminators."

That the same fate did not befall San Antonio's predominantly Tejano population was largely the work of two men: Sam Houston and Juan Seguín. By the end of 1836, Houston returned to Texas as the popular "hero of San Jacinto" and was promptly elected president of the Republic. When President Houston confirmed Seguín as commandant at Béxar in January of 1837, he was directly countermanding an outrageous order that Colonel Seguín had received from one of the most powerful and ambitious newcomers to the Texan military, General Felix Huston.

General Huston (no relation to Sam Houston) had ordered Seguín to depopulate San Antonio and to remove its citizens more than a hundred miles east beyond the Brazos River. Seguín did not obey the order, but appealed directly to the president for relief. Mayor John Linn, who had witnessed similar shenanigans in Victoria, asserted that a group of Anglo "investors" was planning to move in and take over San Antonio as soon as Huston's plan could be put into effect. They abandoned their scheme only when the president's timely revocation of the order was published. As Linn put it, Houston and Seguín had "save[d] the people of [San Antonio]."

A few months later (in May of 1837), the president wisely furloughed most of the unruly Texan volunteer army, which had become the fledgling country's biggest headache as well as the greatest single threat to its Tejano citizens. Felix Huston, who had been cooking up plans of his own for an expedition against Matamoros, went back home to Mississippi.

Although scattered outbreaks of ethnic violence continued, the immediate crisis of the war and its stormy aftermath had passed. For the next decade Texas existed as an independent republic. Juan Seguín was only the most prominent of the Tejanos who participated in the public life of the new nation. Others served in the army and ranger companies; in city councils and the Congress; in jury boxes and even on the bench. (Juan's father, Erasmo Seguín, was named a district court judge by President Houston in 1838.) In 1839, Texas newspapers were explicitly welcoming immigrants from Mexico as well as from Europe and the United States.

For the first half of its existence, the Texas Republic appeared to demonstrate that its brand of "liberty," even if dangerous to Indians and oppressive to blacks, could encompass Anglos and *mexicanos* alike. In a speech to the Texan Senate, Juan Seguín proclaimed that this alliance was a sacred bond of honor and mutual respect, forged in the crucible of war. Yet when the simmering war between Texas and Mexico heated up again in the 1840s, the bond did not hold, and Juan Seguín himself paid the price.

After a Mexican army once again marched north and briefly occupied San Antonio in the spring of 1842, Seguín was falsely accused of treasonably inviting the invasion. Despite the immediate dismissal of these charges by Texan military officials, repeated violent attacks on Seguín and other Tejanos by the undisciplined volunteers who poured into Béxar to "punish the Mexicans" soon forced him to resign as mayor and to flee across the Río Grande—where he was immediately put under arrest as a traitor to Mexico!

Given a choice by the Mexican government between life imprisonment and service with the Mexican army in another symbolic occupation of San Antonio, Seguín chose what he believed to be the course of honor. He returned under arms to his ancestral home in September 1842, offering to assist other Tejanos who might want to accompany him back to exile in Mexico. Demoralized by the abuse they had suffered, hundreds took the opportunity to follow his example. For the Anglos who had driven him out, and for other Texans angered by his apparent apostasy, Seguín became the living symbol of Mexican duplicity and treachery. Thus, even before the United States annexed Texas in 1845 and went to war with Mexico in 1846, relations between Anglos and *mexicanos* in Texas had turned decidedly sour.

The impressive career of Juan Seguín, including his friendship with Sam Houston, was one reason I was so shocked by Houston's speech at Refugio. Shocked but also skeptical. Sam Houston had trusted Juan Seguín enough to confirm him as commandant at San Antonio. ("I entertain for you a high regard, and repose in your honor and chivalry the most implicit confidence," he assured Seguín.) Could the same Houston truly have proclaimed at Refugio that the Anglo "descendants of the sturdy north" could never mix with "the indolent Mexicans, no matter how long we may live among them"? Could *Co-lo-neh*—the

Raven—curse the Mexicans as "half-Indians" and assert that two ethnic groups living together would inevitably produce either enslavement or destruction?

Yet the distinguished historian Paul Lack, in his prize-winning book, *The Texas Revolutionary Experience* (1992), repeatedly cited this speech to support his argument that Houston's blunt words not only showed "the force of the racial antagonism" in his own "long unstated convictions," but also demonstrated that by January 1836 the Revolution "had become a race war" in which "it became virtually inevitable that military authorities would treat all Tejanos as enemies." What was going on? Sure that Paul Lack would never have misquoted Houston, I went to look at my old hero's speech more closely.

In checking the accuracy of the quotation, I saw that Lack had taken the text from the *Papers of the Texas Revolution* (1973), which had in turn copied the speech from the first volume of *The Writings of Sam Houston* (1938). But where had the editors of the *Writings* gotten it? Here's where things got interesting. The transcript had been taken from an unpublished master's thesis completed at the University of Texas in 1925 by Edgar William Bartholomae. When I saw the title of the thesis, I blurted out one word (so loudly that heads turned in the library stacks where I was standing): "EHRENBERG!"

The title of Bartholomae's thesis was: "A Translation of H. Ehrenberg's *Fahrten und Schicksale eines Deutschen in Texas*, with Introduction and Notes." In other words, Bartholomae had produced (under the direction of Eugene C. Barker, by the way) an English version of *Travels and Adventures of a German in Texas*—a lengthy memoir published in Leipzig in the 1840s by Herman

Ehrenberg, who had been a teenaged Prussian volunteer in the Texas Revolution.

The young German had signed up in October of 1835 with the New Orleans Grays—American volunteers who would play leading roles in the Texan struggle. The Grays arrived at the siege of San Antonio just in time to assist in the "Storming of Béxar," and their well-armed presence helped to turn the tide against the numerically superior forces of General Cos. (Ehrenberg's colorful descriptions of legendary Texan heroes "Deaf" Smith and Ben Milam during the action at San Antonio would help to make the twentieth-century English translation of his memoir one of the most often cited eyewitness accounts of the Texas Revolution.)

Following the fall of Béxar to the Texans, Ehrenberg was among the men who followed Frank W. Johnson and Dr. James Grant out of San Antonio to Goliad and then to Refugio. These were the men on the verge of heading toward Matamoros when Sam Houston arrived in January 1836 to try to stop them. As we have seen, the volunteers would not turn back, and consented only to wait for reinforcements from their other new commander, Colonel James W. Fannin. Ehrenberg was among the handful of volunteers sent to meet Fannin's supply ships when they arrived on the South Texas coast around the first of February.

When Fannin learned at Refugio of threatening movements of the Mexican army along the Río Grande, he urged the volunteers to fall back with him to the fortress at Goliad and to strengthen it against attack. Most of the men complied, but Johnson and Grant rejected Fannin's cautious course, and with a splinter group they prepared to head south. Separated even from each other and with their forces fatally split, both Johnson and Grant were each quickly surprised and defeated by advancing Mexican troops under General José Urrea. Grant and more than half of his men were killed; only six avoided capture. Of Johnson's larger group, only the hapless "commander" and four others escaped to bring word of the disaster to Fannin at Goliad. Houston's fears were becoming a reality—but the worst was yet to come.

After Colonel Fannin learned on February 25 that Santa Anna had surrounded and laid siege to the Alamo, he made a half-hearted attempt to march there in relief, but abandoned the effort when his wagons broke down no more than two miles from Goliad. His men returned to hold and fortify the presidio.

Yet Fannin risked much just by staying at Goliad, for if the Alamo fell to Santa Anna, Fannin would find himself outflanked. Retreat to a more defensible position on the Guadalupe River at Victoria became advisable, yet Fannin could not bring himself to leave the fortress his men had worked so hard to make ready. And when news of the Alamo's fall arrived in Goliad along with a positive order to retreat from General Houston (who had finally been given command over all Texan forces), Fannin's forces were fatally divided and unready to move out.

Responding to a frantic request for assistance from straggling colonists in Refugio, Fannin had unwisely dispatched most of his carts and wagons with a small force directly into the path of General Urrea's army. When this force ran into trouble, the impulsive Fannin sent a third of his remaining men into the maelstrom. Soon they were all either dead, captured, or desperate fugitives trying to elude Urrea's lancers.

Only when it was too late, on March 19, did Fannin begin the retreat from the Goliad presidio, which he had vainly renamed "Fort Defiance." Herman Ehrenberg's memoir vividly recounts the tragedy that followed: the Texans were overtaken on an open plain, where they battled valiantly but had no choice but to surrender to General Urrea's superior force. The prisoners—over three hundred in all—were returned to Goliad and crowded into the presidio's small chapel. Here they suffered severely from a lack of water during their first night of captivity. For the next two days water was all they received—and when they were finally thrown cuts of freshly killed beef, they had no way to cook the meat except by tearing wood panels from the chapel walls and lighting smoky fires in the cramped quarters. Ehrenberg gulped down his portion raw.

After being held in the presidio for a week (they were allowed to sleep on the grounds only after three excruciating nights in the chapel), Ehrenberg and his comrades were led out of the fort on Palm Sunday (March 27) in three groups, all told that they were being deported to New Orleans by way of Matamoros. But Ehrenberg grew suspicious when he saw that his Mexican guards were in dress uniforms and not carrying their field equipment—hardly what one would expect at the beginning of a two-hundred-mile march. Moreover, each of the three groups was marched in a different direction.

No more than fifteen minutes from the presidio, as Ehrenberg's party neared the San Antonio River, the command was given to halt. At about the same time, Ehrenberg heard musket fire in the distance. By this time the guards had raised their guns and were aiming at the prisoners' chests from three paces away.

Then the men were ordered to kneel. Another sound of distant muskets was heard, this time mixed with impassioned shouts. As the Texans realized at last what was happening to them, the guards fired. Ehrenberg heard the "loud crackling noise" of the muskets, "and then there was nothing but silence."

The two men on either side of Ehrenberg fell mortally wounded, but the bullets missed the teenager and in the ensuing smoke and confusion he ran for the river, escaping with his life. After several days of wandering and almost starving, he was recaptured by other units of the Mexican army, who placed him on a work detail with other prisoners. In the chaos that followed Santa Anna's defeat at San Jacinto, he escaped a second time and finally reached elements of Houston's victorious army. After all this travel and adventure, Ehrenberg accepted an honorable discharge from the Texan service and eventually made his way back to Germany, where his eyewitness account of the "war for freedom in Texas" became a best seller.

Ehrenberg was a great storyteller, but was he reliable? I had read the typescript of Bartholomae's translation many years earlier, in the basement of the library of the University of Texas in Austin. For some reason, my most vivid recollection from the memoir was of Ehrenberg's overheated description of some bizarre characters in a Mexican coffeehouse and gambling den in Nacogdoches that he had visited with his comrades from the New Orleans Grays. I had a hunch Ehrenberg might be prone to embellishment.

Yet his memoir had become a favorite source for historians of the Texas Revolution, especially after an English translation by Charlotte Churchill was published in 1935, under the title

*With Milam and Fannin: Adventures of a German Boy in Texas'
Revolution.* Puzzled at how I could have failed to notice the thrust
of Houston's speech in my previous readings of Ehrenberg, I
turned to this edition to see how Churchill had translated the offending remarks.

Now I was really stunned—the words were not there! The beginning and ending of Houston's speech were translated, but the
"racist" heart—the "indolent Mexicans," the "half-Indians," the
flying tomahawks and scalping knives—all of that had been cut
out!

My curiosity aroused, I flipped back to read Churchill's
translated description of the New Orleans Grays' stopover in
Nacogdoches—and their visit to that Mexican coffeehouse I so
clearly remembered. The entire "Coffee-*Haus*" chapter was gone
without a trace! At this point, I dug out the yellowing notes that
I had taken on Bartholomae's thesis almost twenty years earlier
during my dissertation research on Anglo-Texan racial attitudes.
When I compared my notes to the published text, I found that
virtually all of the anti-Mexican comments from Ehrenberg's
memoir were missing from the Churchill translation. My inquiry
into Paul Lack's sources was quickly turning into a piece of detective work.

I ordered the Bartholomae typescript from the University of
Texas through interlibrary loan, and also secured a microfilm of
Ehrenberg's original German edition. Over the Christmas holi-
days of 1992 and into the new year, I compared, paragraph by
paragraph, the three Ehrenberg texts. To my amazement, there
were almost seventy separate deletions of text in the Churchill
volume, from whole chapters and paragraphs to individual words

that were apparently deemed offensive—as when all references to sex, alcohol, and even billiards were removed!

As I expected, the master's thesis was a complete translation, but clumsy. It became apparent that Bartholomae was working in haste, and was not completely proficient in reading the old-style German "Fraktur" typeface used in the original Leipzig printings of Ehrenberg's book. Numerous mistranslations were the result, and some of these reversed the original meaning of the text—masking Ehrenberg's actual ideas almost as completely as did the intentional censorship of Churchill's text.

For instance, Bartholomae mistook "*Feigheit*" (cowardice) for "*Freiheit*" (freedom), with the result that Ehrenberg's original statement, that "the brown inhabitants of Mexico . . . are characterized by their cowardice" became the quite different assertion that the Mexicans "cherish their independence." In another case, the misreading of the letter *h* as *f* in the German word *Phlegma* transformed Mexico's "sluggishness" into that country's *Pflegma*, a nonexistent word that the harried graduate student imaginatively translated as "recuperative power"! With these and similar errors obscuring the author's own ideas and opinions, even those few historians who sought out the obscure Bartholomae thesis might be excused for not recognizing Ehrenberg's fingerprints on the words of the speech he attributed to Sam Houston.

But the fingerprints are there, in the midst of even more lapses by Bartholomae. The "Houston" speech excerpted earlier in this chapter includes a very odd reference to a "live slab" of cactus. In advocating Texan independence, Houston was quoted as saying: "let us break off the live slab from the dying cactus that it may not dry up with the remainder; let us plant it anew that it may spring luxuriantly out of the fruitful savannah." In translating this passage (which does not appear at all in the published Churchill version) Bartholomae unfortunately failed to notice the helpful footnote that Ehrenberg had provided for his German readers: "The Mexican escutcheon [or coat of arms] is a cactus [of the prickly pear type] with as many leaves [or sections] as states to be found in the [Mexican] federation." Had he seen this explanation, Bartholomae might not have misread *Blatt* (leaf) for *Platt[e]* (slab), and thus put into circulation a garbled statement that caused Paul Lack to observe that "Houston resorted to a bundle of mixed metaphors to emphasize the force of [his] racial antagonism" toward Mexicans.

In fact, what the passage displays is Bartholomae's mistranslation of Ehrenberg's dubious recollection. The metaphor of the replanted cactus leaf is much more likely Ehrenberg's own than Houston's. In another section of the memoir omitted from the Churchill edition, Ehrenberg repeats the allusion to Texas as a replanted leaf of the Mexican cactus, this time as if he himself had uttered the phrase, in an alleged (and highly unlikely) political debate between himself (as a captive) and the Mexican General José Urrea.

A thorough comparison of Ehrenberg's memoir with the voluminous surviving writings of Sam Houston reveals that the vocabulary, the metaphors, and most importantly, the beliefs and ideas of the infamous speech are those of the German private, and not of the Texan general. There is little doubt that in January 1836 Sam Houston gave a speech at Refugio in which he argued against the wisdom of an attack on Matamoros, but this does not make him an anti-Mexican racist. Houston's actions speak far louder than Ehrenberg's unsubstantiated words.

As we have seen, upon becoming president of the Republic of Texas, Houston not only thwarted those in the army who continued to push for an offensive into Mexico, but also acted firmly to reverse a vicious cycle of ethnic polarization that had threatened to overwhelm Texas in the aftermath of the Revolution. He countermanded Felix Huston's orders to evacuate San Antonio, and placed in loyal Tejano hands (those of the Seguíns) the highest military and judicial posts of the Texas Republic on its exposed western frontier.

"Ehrenberg," as a fellow named Henry Smith put it, "had a regrettable tendency to write florid speeches and put them into the mouths of historic personages." This was not the opinion of the cantankerous Texan provisional governor by the same name, but a very different Henry Smith: the Dallas-based editor of Charlotte Churchill's 1935 translation of Ehrenberg, *With Milam and Fannin.*

Churchill's book, not Bartholomae's thesis, was responsible for introducing Ehrenberg to most students (and teachers) of Texas history. For more than sixty years, it was the *only* published English translation. Its deletion of almost seventy offensive passages from the original German made it difficult for anyone to trace the racist language attributed to Sam Houston back to Herman Ehrenberg himself. The fingerprints had vanished, along with the language. In the meantime, the offensive language attributed to Houston found its way into the historical mainstream when the editors of *The Writings of Sam Houston* copied Ehrenberg's words (in English) from Bartholomae's thesis.

As the editor of Churchill's translation, Henry Smith was responsible for many of the deletions—those passages that Smith considered "unhistorical" or otherwise unreliable (such as the alleged debate between Ehrenberg and Urrea). In addition, the book's Dallas publisher, William Tardy, eliminated or rewrote many more passages that he considered unsuitable for children, in an effort to assure that the book would be adopted by the Texas public schools during the 1936 centennial celebration of Texan independence.

The final bowdlerized result was an embarrassment even to Henry Smith. He erased *With Milam and Fannin* from his own résumé—and essentially from his entire life. So thoroughly had his own fingerprints been removed that after he became famous by his full name of Henry Nash Smith for writing the classic, *Virgin Land: The American West as Symbol and Myth* (1950), no one made the connection between the distinguished literary scholar and the obscure young editor from Dallas. At least not until I tried to discover, in 1993, the identity of this self-effacing editor. By coincidence, that year was the bicentennial of Houston's birth, and Old Sam was already catching flak in the press for his alleged 1836 attack on the Tejanos. I was glad that I could help to set the record straight.

Yet there was more to this affair than discovering the true author of the speech, or even of preserving Sam Houston's reputation. For more than a century, either race or racism has been at the center of virtually every explanation of the origin of the Texas Revolution. In 1938, when Ehrenberg's version of Houston's plea to the soldiers at Refugio appeared in the respected *Writings of Sam Houston*, co-edited by the eminent Eugene C.

Barker, such anti-Mexican sentiments came as no surprise to most readers—and no one gave a thought to pursuing the source of the speech for errors. Even in 1992, Paul Lack was convinced that these words revealed Houston's "long unstated convictions" and the "force of [his] racial antagonism."

Sam Houston and Juan Seguín had in fact worked against the forces of racism both during the revolt and in the republic that they helped to create. But the ethnic prejudices that stained that republic also came to blot out an essential part of the history of Texas. "Remember the Alamo" became a formula for forgetfulness. The voices of Seguín and his men from Béxar were all but silenced; for decades the Tejanos were virtually erased from standard histories of the war against Mexico and from the historical memories of most Texans. I was in graduate school before I had ever heard of Juan Seguín. And even when a good historian such as Paul Lack strove to set the record straight and to tell the story whole, he found Ehrenberg's distorted image of Sam Houston more convincing than the man's actual words and deeds. What else might lie hidden in these deafening silences or behind these blinding orthodoxies?

When I sent to press in the summer of 1993 an article outlining my findings about Ehrenberg and Houston ("Sam Houston's Speechwriters: The Grad Student, the Teenager, the Editors, and the Historians"), my editor at the *Southwestern Historical Quarterly* informed me that another detective was also at work rewriting the history of the Texas Revolution. Bill Groneman—a real detective from the arson squad of the New York City Fire Department—was in his spare time focusing his attention on the fateful events surrounding the most famous battle of the Texas Revolution: the valiant last stand at the Alamo in March 1836. Both Groneman and I were too busy with our own projects to make contact in 1993. But shortly after our paths crossed on the grounds of the Alamo the following year, I found myself pursuing another mystery—and smack in the middle of an incendiary controversy over just what had happened in the last moments of the Battle of the Alamo.

· Two ·

WITH SANTA ANNA IN TEXAS

I SHOULD HAVE KNOWN WHO HE WAS WHEN HE WALKED INTO the room. Although we were in San Antonio, the "Noo Yawk" accent was unmistakable when the stranger asked to see the Chief Archivist. I was sitting in the reading room of the Library of the Daughters of the Republic of Texas, a haven of historical research half-hidden from the tourists in a shaded corner of the Alamo grounds. There were plenty of sightseers around, however, because the day before—March 6, 1994—had been the anniversary of the final, deadly assault on the old mission in 1836 by the overwhelming forces of General Santa Anna.

There didn't have to be a fight here in 1836. Sam Houston had sent Jim Bowie to Béxar in January of that year with the hope that Bowie would persuade the volunteers at the Alamo to quit the place. Never designed as a fortress, incapable of protecting the town of San Antonio from occupation by the enemy, commanding no strategic pass through which Santa Anna would have to march, and far removed from the Anglo-American settlements in Texas, the Alamo appeared to Houston to be nothing more than a trap for anyone who would dare defend it.

But defend it Bowie determined to do. He wrote to Governor Henry Smith on February 2 that he was ready to "die in these ditches" rather than give up the rebel outpost. Smith agreed, but could provide little support. He ordered Lieutenant Colonel William Barret Travis to raise a company to reinforce the Alamo, but only thirty men responded to the call. Travis threatened to resign his commission rather than lead such a tiny force, but in the end he complied. When he and his troopers arrived at the Alamo, they found an ungainly structure enclosing a central *plaza* of almost three acres, defended by barely a hundred men. At least four times that number would be needed to operate the Alamo's big guns and to man its lengthy walls. Not even the famous Davy Crockett, who showed up on February 8 with a handful of Tennessee volunteers, could make up for the critical shortage of manpower.

When Colonel James C. Neill, the officer in charge of the garrison, was compelled to depart in mid-February to attend a family stricken with illness, clashes of personality threatened to split those who remained at the Alamo. Neill attempted to hand over command to Travis, but volunteers who favored Bowie demanded the right to choose their own commander. They prevailed, and, as their new leader celebrated his election with a "roaring drunk," Travis was again ready to walk away from this assignment. But a powerful hangover brought Bowie to his senses, and the two men finally agreed on a joint command.

There was no time to lose. Reports were already coming in from Juan Seguín's mounted Tejano scouts that the Mexican army had crossed the Río Grande. Travis discounted these stories as exaggerations, but on February 23 a large force under Santa Anna himself surprised the rebels by marching into San Antonio from the west. The Texans lounging in town barely had time to grab a few provisions and fall back into the Alamo. Bowie suggested a parley with the enemy, but Travis answered the Mexicans' demand for unconditional surrender with a cannon shot. Further disagreement between the Alamo's commanders vanished, however, when Bowie fell deathly ill on the second day of the siege.

For the next ten days, Travis watched the noose tighten around him. Juan Seguín, James Bonham, and other couriers who slipped through the Mexican lines to find reinforcements produced paltry results. The thirty-odd volunteers from Gonzales who appeared under the walls at three o'clock in the morning on the first of March were all (that we know for certain) who came to Travis's aid—though perhaps as many as sixty more (according to Mexican body-counts) arrived in time to become unknown martyrs. Colonel James W. Fannin's half-hearted effort to come to the rescue ended, as we have seen, in a fiasco of broken-down wagons and wandering oxen.

The remarkable thing is that Santa Anna decided to assault the Alamo at all. The few men in the fort could be easily bypassed and cut off from the rest of the Texan forces. Even if Travis wanted a battle, Santa Anna did not have to take the bait. But the Mexican commander in chief wanted vengeance and glory. A spectacular victory at the very scene of General Cos's December disgrace was the kind of news that Santa Anna wanted to send back to Mexico City, where military victories were the surest guarantee of his political survival.

The actual Battle of the Alamo was almost an anticlimax. After pounding the Texans with a constant bombardment for almost two weeks, Santa Anna ordered his guns to cease firing on the night of March 5. The mass assault on the walls, which came the next day before dawn, was twice turned back by deadly Texan firepower before the sheer force of Mexican numbers overcame all resistance. The battle was over in less than an hour. Every Texan defender of the Alamo died, but because their cause was ultimately victorious, the Texan fighters passed from life into legend.

Travis wrote his way into the Texan pantheon of heroes, penning phrases in his letters from the Alamo that reverberate even today:

> [O]ur flag still waves proudly from the walls. *I shall never surrender or retreat. . . .* I am determined to sustain myself as long as possible & die like a soldier who never forgets what is due his own honor & that of his country. VICTORY OR DEATH.

Bowie and Bonham also achieved heroic status through the way they faced the end: Bowie exhorting the Alamo defenders even from his deathbed and Bonham galloping back into the doomed fortress on March 3 only to report that Fannin would not be bringing relief from Goliad.

David Crockett rounded out what became the Alamo's fabulous four. With the exception of President Andrew Jackson, Crockett was the most celebrated man in North America even before he rode into San Antonio: he was known as champion bear-hunter, homespun humorist, and outspoken (ex-)congressman from the backwoods. Virginian John Sowers Brooks (one of

Herman Ehrenberg's fellow-soldiers at Goliad), upon learning that Crockett was among those who repulsed an early Mexican probe of the Alamo's defenses, wrote his mother that "Probably Davy Crockett 'grinned them off'"—just as Crockett had once boasted that he could grin down an angry bear.

No defender survived who saw Davy Crockett die at the Alamo, and conflicting versions of his last moments were circulating within weeks of the battle. Few in my generation, who had watched Fess Parker swinging his rifle as the television screen faded to black in 1955, doubted that Crockett fell in desperate combat. But in the ensuing decades cynicism and historical revisionism had taken a toll on such certainties. That's why I was so interested in the gentleman from New York who had come to San Antonio on the anniversary of Crockett's death.

Bill Groneman, a New York City detective, was in the Alamo city to sign copies of his new book, *Defense of a Legend: Crockett and the de la Peña Diary.* This was the much-anticipated work that my editor had mentioned to me the previous summer, and the latest chapter in one of the most intense historical controversies of recent times. The diary of José Enrique de la Peña, a Mexican officer who marched into Texas with Santa Anna in 1836, was notorious for a single paragraph describing an "unpleasant episode" that had allegedly occurred only a few yards from where I was sitting in the library's quiet reading room. De la Peña claimed to be an eyewitness to the capture and execution of David Crockett in the immediate aftermath of the Battle of the Alamo.

Groneman's book, I soon learned, was an all-out assault on the de la Peña diary, not merely on its accuracy, but on its very authenticity. After I had introduced myself to him, Bill showed me the cover of his new volume and bluntly announced its central thesis: the famous "diary" was a probable forgery.

It was difficult to concentrate on my own research after Groneman left the library. As soon as it closed its doors for the day at five o'clock, I hurried across the street toward the bookstore where Groneman was still signing copies of *Defense of a Legend*. I bought one on the spot.

Thumbing through my newly autographed copy, I was impressed. Not only did Groneman claim that the de la Peña manuscript contained telltale anachronisms indicating a forgery, but he had even provided a photograph of the suspected culprit! The suave old gentleman with the charming smile and the twinkling eyes was identified as John A. Laflin, "one of the greatest forgers in American history." From the 1940s until his death in 1970, Laflin (among other escapades) had repeatedly tried to pass himself off as the great-grandson of Jean Lafitte, the pirate who had plied the coastal waters of Texas and Louisiana, at times smuggling slaves in concert with Jim Bowie.

Even more impressive was Groneman's published photocopy of a "Certification" from the famed handwriting expert Charles Hamilton, who had devoted a whole chapter to Laflin in his 1980 book, *Great Forgers and Famous Fakes*. Hamilton's signed statement was unequivocal: "I have carefully examined the document allegedly written by JOSE ENRIQUE DE LA PENA, entitled PERSONAL NARRATIVE WITH SANTA ANNA IN TEXAS, and find that it is a forgery by John Laflin, alias John Laffite."

Groneman's book was obviously a bombshell, a major event in a war of words over Crockett's death that had become much

John A. Laffite, a.k.a. John A. Laflin. (COPYRIGHT: SAM HOUSTON RE-
GIONAL LIBRARY AND RESEARCH CENTER, LIBERTY, TEXAS.)

more vicious in the late twentieth century than it had ever been
in the years immediately following the fall of the Alamo. Newspaper reports in the spring and summer of 1836 varied wildly as
to the circumstances of Crockett's demise, ranging from glow-
ing reports of his fighting like a tiger until the bitter end to de-

scriptions of his brutal execution along with a handful of other prisoners on the express orders of General Santa Anna.

For the next century, several competing (and largely undocumented) versions of Crockett's final moments coexisted, but many who celebrated the memory of this most prominent "martyr of the Alamo" seemed untroubled by the conflicting details. As late as 1934, a popular edition of *The Adventures of Davy Crockett* (published by Charles Scribner's Sons) featured as its frontispiece a portrayal of the captive Alamo defender painted by the Texan artist and decorated U.S. Marine John W. Thomason, Jr., a military hero in his own right. Hands tied behind his back, Thomason's Crockett is being led to stand before Santa Anna.

When Scribner's brought out a new edition of this book in 1955, however, the graphic depiction of captivity had vanished. What had changed? A cultural critic might argue that in the midst of the Cold War, the example of a Crockett who had allowed himself to be captured alive by the forces of tyranny conflicted with the dominant American doctrine that even nuclear war was preferable to conquest by the enemy: "better dead than Red."

A more immediate reason for dropping the disturbing image may have been fact that the book's re-issue came in the midst of the same "Davy Crockett craze" that sent me with my coonskin cap into my own backyard Alamo. The final fade-out notwithstanding, there was no doubt that Walt Disney's Davy went down swinging. John Wayne's portrayal of Crockett fighting to the death in the 1960 movie *The Alamo* reinforced this heroic image in the collective memory of mid-twentieth-century Americans.

Ironically, it was in precisely the years 1955 and 1960 that the two most important eyewitness accounts of Crockett's death,

"Crockett led before Santa Anna" by John W. Thomason, Jr. (COPY-
RIGHT: DR. T.C. COLE, JR. PHOTOGRAPH COURTESY OF THE CENTER FOR AMER-
ICAN HISTORY, UNIVERSITY OF TEXAS AT AUSTIN.)

each ostensibly narrated by a Mexican soldier, came to light—far apart and under very different circumstances. Each account presented a Davy Crockett that more closely matched the captive figure drawn by John Thomason than the ones portrayed by Fess Parker or John Wayne.

The extensive de la Peña manuscripts were acquired from unknown sources by J. Sánchez Garza, a dealer in antiquities who edited and privately published them from his home in Mexico City in 1955 as *La Rebelión de Texas: Manuscrito Inédito de 1836 por un Oficial de Santa Anna.* A second narrative of Crockett's execution, now known as the "Dolson Letter," was accidentally discovered by a Rice University graduate student in the 1836 files of the (Detroit) *Democratic Free Press* and published in the *Journal of Southern History* in August 1960. (The Dolson Letter will be discussed in detail in the following chapter.)

The immediate impact of Sánchez Garza's publication of the de la Peña papers on either Texan historiography or the American historical consciousness was virtually nil. In *Thirteen Days to Glory*, a perennially popular history of the Alamo battle published in 1958, author Lon Tinkle called the Mexican diary one of "the most interesting contributions to Alamo investigation in recent years," but it's unlikely that Tinkle had even seen, much less read, the book. In his bibliographical section he failed to mention the title and incorrectly listed both the date of publication and the diarist's name (he called him "Gonzalez Pena"). Tinkle labeled the book's contents as "vitriolic," probably because of its criticism of Mexican generals and politicians, but he made no reference to de la Peña's version of Crockett's death.

Three years later, Walter Lord prominently featured de la Peña's testimony in a section titled "Did David Crockett Surrender?" in his far superior book on the Alamo, *A Time to Stand*. Yet there was barely a ripple of public notice. Lord himself perhaps lessened the impact of his revelation when he stressed that despite the contemporary evidence of the execution—he listed also the Dolson Letter, the newspaper accounts, and some secondhand testimony from Mexican prisoners of war—most early Texas accounts (though none by eyewitnesses) flatly declared that Crockett fell in battle. Lord certainly hedged his conclusion, noting that, while "it's just possible" that Crockett surrendered, "there's a good chance that [he] lived up to his legend."

De la Peña's narrative was cited in a few obscure works written by Spanish-speaking authors in the 1960s, but nothing for the remainder of that decade altered the sense that both this Mexican officer and the story that he told were still figuratively covered by the dust of forgetfulness (*el polvo del olvido*) from which the antiquarian Sánchez Garza had tried to rescue the man and his memoir.

The dust (*polvo*) turned out to be gunpowder (*pólvora*). A delayed (and quite unexpected) explosion occurred in 1975 when the Texas A&M University Press unveiled *With Santa Anna in Texas: A Personal Narrative of the Revolution, by José Enrique de la Peña*. The perpetrators had not intended to be bomb-throwers. Carmen Perry, a former director of the Daughters of the Republic of Texas Library at the Alamo, had been engaged to translate the de la Peña manuscripts by John R. Peace, a prominent Texan attorney and politician instrumental in the creation of the University of Texas at San Antonio (UTSA). Peace, Perry, and UTSA librarian Michael Kelly had earlier traveled together to Mexico City to arrange the purchase of the bundle of old papers from the widow of J. Sánchez Garza. Although Carmen Perry eventually received academic accolades for her work, the immediate rewards for her labors were tabloid headlines, hate mail, and midnight phone calls from people who could not tolerate the thought of a helpless and submissive Crockett.

A similar fate awaited Dan Kilgore, an accountant and avocational historian from Corpus Christi. His 1977 presidential address to the Texas State Historical Association—published the next year as *How Did Davy Die?*—meticulously examined the questions raised by Perry's publication and came down solidly on the side of de la Peña rather than Disney. For his troubles, Kilgore was branded by irate respondents as a "mealy-mouthed intellectual" and a "smut peddler" who should have his mouth washed out with soap. Retaining the Cold War rhetoric of the 1950s, a writer from Ft. Myers, Florida, told Kilgore (a conservative Republican) that his book was "one of the Communits [*sic*] plans to degrade our hero's" [*sic*], and added, echoing the famous ballad of the Disneyland Crockett, "He's still King of the wild frontier." What Kilgore had envisioned as an academic exercise in the interpretation of documentary evidence became instead a case study in the power of myth.

Although the ranting and raving "crazies" received most of the attention of those who have revisited the Crockett controversy of the 1970s, Bill Groneman perceptively noted in *Defense of a Legend* that the responses of these "kooks" had been stimulated by the tremendous press coverage given Crockett's alleged surrender at that time. This media frenzy, along with the increasing (and uncritical) scholarly acceptance of the de la Peña version of the events, were, Groneman believed, signs of the times. In the political and social atmosphere of the mid-1970s, he argued, a generation of Americans disillusioned by Vietnam and Watergate found it far harder than ever before to celebrate "the image of Crockett clubbing away at hoards [*sic*] of swarthy men," and far easier than ever before to accept a cynically revisionist image of Crockett as a "sly politician" who tried to talk his way out of trouble when caught by the Mexicans in the Alamo.

Groneman also pointed to the inhibitions that may have prevented some of those doubters, like himself, from speaking out in dissent: a desire to avoid being lumped with the "kooks who harassed Perry and Kilgore" and qualms about being seen as irrational defenders of "childhood heroes." Groneman also claimed that there was a fear of being branded as a "racist . . . if you did not believe the de la Peña account." Moreover, said this dedicated amateur historian, many of those who swallowed their doubts did so because it was simply unthinkable that the "serious historians" who endorsed the de la Peña version did not know "what they were talking about."

By 1994 Groneman was ready to cast aside these inhibitions and challenge the reliability of the de la Peña diary. For me, his determination seemed admirable, especially in light of my recent experience with the bogus "Sam Houston speech." I put *Defense of a Legend* on the top of my summer reading list—a temptation that soon became a duty when George Ward, my editor at the *Southwestern Historical Quarterly*, asked if I would review the book. I leaped to the task, expecting to write a quick and positive analysis of the work of a fellow historical detective who had gone back to the original sources to set the record straight. But that's not exactly what I found.

Bill had indeed uncovered problems with the diary. He easily put his finger on the most obvious discrepancy: the same professional historians who had uncritically endorsed the de la Peña diary as the "best" and "most reliable" source for the death of Crockett had also stated unequivocally that it had been published in 1836—and that was simply impossible! It could not have happened because buried deep in de la Peña's narrative is a reference to the published diary of another Mexican officer, General José Urrea—and Urrea's *Diario* was not published until 1838. Obviously, any narrative containing this reference could not have existed, much less have been published, in 1836.

The presence of this apparent anachronism was clearly Groneman's strongest argument against the authenticity of the de la Peña diary. His other points were weaker. It was true, as he said, that there was no clear provenance for these manuscripts—they appeared as if by magic in the hands of J. Sánchez Garza, who offered no explanation for their origin. But many valuable historical documents have turned up in unlikely places, and with no paper trail leading back to their creators. Moreover, Groneman's charges that John Laflin had forged the manuscripts, perhaps in concert with Sánchez Garza, appeared upon close examination to be convenient conjectures rather than convincing proofs. Finally, the examples given by Groneman of "similar language" in the de la Peña manuscripts and various documents from a later time (including some allegedly forged by Laflin), were inconclusive. There were some vaguely similar *ideas*, but the words didn't match.

Even Groneman's strongest point was not enough to close what I had expected to be an open-and-shut case of forgery. Groneman's argument that the alleged forger had carelessly committed an anachronism could be expressed as a logical syllogism, with two related factual premises and a necessary conclusion.

Premise One: this is a document "purported to have been written and published in 1836." *Premise Two*: the document contains material (the reference to Urrea's publication) that could have been written no earlier than 1838. *Conclusion*: the diary must be a fraud. The problem was that Groneman had quoted no original source in establishing his first premise. Did the diary itself claim to have been produced in 1836? I couldn't tell from reading Groneman's book, and I could not imagine why he would not have included that information if it existed. Curious, I picked up a copy of *With Santa Anna in Texas*, Carmen Perry's translation.

Her "Translator's Preface" did not resolve the mystery, but instead deepened it. "The narrative translated here," Perry wrote, "is de la Peña's own presentation of his diary. Though it incorporates observations on the conduct and particulars of the campaign which he made later on, he took great care to distinguish these from the diary itself, which he presents just as it was written in the field." Perry noted that the manuscripts brought back from Mexico included not only the narrative text that she had translated in full, but also "all the field notes and the original holograph diary." Thus she had been able to compare the diary as originally written with de la Peña's later "presentation" of it. But how much later had de la Peña written his additional observations?

Perry gave no direct answer, but hinted that they were completed only a few months after the Texas campaign had come to an end. She noted that the 1955 Mexico City edition produced by J. Sánchez Garza contained "a title page which purports to be from an edition of the de la Peña diary printed in September, 1836, in Matamoros, Tam[auli]p[a]s, Mexico." She added, however, that "no copy of this edition could be located either in Mexico or the United States." Perry offered an explanation: "If indeed this edition ever appeared, it is possible that most or all copies of it were destroyed because of the highly critical nature of its contents."

Historian Llerena Friend, who wrote an introduction to Perry's 1975 translation, was aware of the anomalous reference to Urrea's book lurking in the translated text and hazarded a guess that, since Urrea's book had actually quoted anonymous passages from de la Peña's diary, perhaps at some point there had been an exchange of manuscripts between the two men. However, this would not explain how de la Peña, writing in 1836, could discuss the publication of Urrea's *Diario* in 1838. The pesky anachronism would neither fully reveal itself nor go away.

At this point, I had little choice but to press on to examine the translated narrative itself. What was in "the original diary," and what had been added later? How much later? Was there, or could there have been, an 1836 edition of de la Peña's diary that had been eradicated from existence? Perhaps de la Peña himself could provide some answers.

Reseña y Diario

de

LA CAMPAÑA DE TEXAS

Por

JOSE ENRIQUE DE LA PEÑA

Matamoros, Tamps.

Septiembre 15 de 1836

"Title Page" of de la Peña's Memoir (published 1955). (COURTESY OF
THE CENTER FOR AMERICAN HISTORY, UNIVERSITY OF TEXAS AT AUSTIN.)

The Mexican officer's most direct statements seemed to confirm Groneman's analysis. A four-page prologue consisted of a letter de la Peña wrote to a colleague on September 15, 1836. In it, he outlined "the principal causes which compelled me to publish the diary I kept during the time I served in this unfortunate campaign, and at the same time to make a brief review of what is written there. . . . I could have published my notes a few days after I returned from the campaign, but I was convinced that in order to be impartial, I had to take some time to verify those acts to which I was not an eyewitness and to obtain more accurate information about others, important objectives which I achieved by collecting the daybooks from the various sections that constituted the army." Apparently de la Peña took two or three months in the summer of 1836—his published narrative ends on June 11—to collect these materials and complete his expanded "presentation" of the diary.

This assumption seems to be confirmed by an unequivocal statement on the very last page of the Perry translation. After ending his narrative with the words, "Mexicans, there are the facts. Judge for yourselves, and let your terrible verdict fall upon those who may deserve it," de la Peña wrote, "I have concluded this narrative during the most pressing moments, a few hours before resuming the march, as I have already been informed about San Luis." Both this statement and the prologue appear to be signed and dated by de la Peña in Matamoros on September 15, 1836.

It is a puzzle. If the narrative is genuine, how the devil did that reference to General Urrea's 1838 publication get into the text? And if it is a fraud, how could the perpetrator of such an elaborate hoax, after taking great care to emphasize the document's origin in 1836, have been so stupid as to put the blatant 1838 reference into his carefully constructed forgery? There were almost two hundred pages of diary entries and commentary between the first and last pages of *With Santa Anna in Texas*—would they reveal an answer to either of these questions? As is often the case in historical work, the answers that the narrative provided were subtle, indirect, and contextual rather than direct and to the point. I began to study, page by page, the story de la Peña told.

The deeper I plunged into his account, the more I felt I was reading the work of a genuine personality rather than a forger's attempt to construct a work that could slip neatly into the gaps in the existing literature. From the point of view of this Mexican captain (who received a field commission as a lieutenant colonel at the start of the Texas campaign), there were far more important issues involved in this war than the death of David Crockett. De la Peña was an angry young man, much more angry with the Mexican political and military establishment than with the Texan rebels who had dismembered his country. Forgetting Davy Crockett for the moment, I was soon drawn into "de la Peña's war."

De la Peña did not oppose the campaign against the rebels in Texas—it was necessary, he believed, in order to prevent not only dismemberment but also dishonor for the Mexican nation. There was great anguish felt within the army when General Cos was defeated at San Antonio in December 1835 and forced to withdraw across the Río Grande. It was this humiliation, de la Peña suggested, that led to the disaster at the Alamo—and because of the needless loss of life among Santa Anna's troops, he considered the Alamo a disaster for the Mexican army even more than for the Texans!

Marching overland from central Mexico to San Antonio de Béxar in the dead of winter, wrote de la Peña, was quite unnecessary militarily. He believed that Santa Anna's anger and shame over Cos's capitulation had turned the recapture of Béxar into an urgent priority for psychological rather than strategic reasons. Santa Anna had dispatched General Urrea with roughly a third of the total Mexican invasion force of over six thousand men with orders to move north from Matamoros against the rebels serving under Johnson, Grant, and Fannin. The commander in chief kept the big prize for himself, however. To retake San Antonio, the historic capital of Texas, was an essential step in erasing the stain left by Cos's defeat. And it was clear that Santa Anna's solvent for the stain would be blood.

As Santa Anna marched north into Coahuila in 1835, his Minister of War, José María Tornel, issued a decree on December 30 declaring that armed expeditions were being sent into Mexico from the United States to aid the Texan rebels, and warning that in response the Mexican nation was authorizing commanders in the field to punish as pirates any foreigners who carried or shipped arms into the country for purposes of aiding the rebellion. Santa Anna would use the "Tornel Decree" to justify the summary execution of anyone captured bearing arms against the central Mexican government.

Moreover, just before the assault on the Alamo, when the issue of the treatment of potential prisoners came up at a conference of officers, de la Peña overheard Santa Anna invoke the example of the Spanish General Joaquín de Arredondo, who brutally crushed a rebellion against Spain in San Antonio in 1813: "he had hanged eight hundred or more . . . and this conduct was taken as a model." As a young officer serving under Arredondo at the time, Santa Anna had been impressed by the political effectiveness of his chief's draconian methods. Unlike Santa Anna, de la Peña believed that such measures against the enemy would be both unnecessary and counterproductive in the campaign of 1836, but it was the shedding of Mexican blood even more than that of defeated Americans and Texans that caused de la Peña to despise Santa Anna's generalship.

When the final assault took place in the early morning of March 6, de la Peña lost many friends among the scores of soldiers mowed down as they stormed the Alamo walls—a costly tactic that would have been unnecessary if Santa Anna had waited for the arrival a few days later of his heavy artillery. Santa Anna's forced march across Coahuila in January and February had indeed surprised the Texans, but the rapid progress by the Mexican foot soldiers had outpaced the army's slower-moving large cannons (capable of hurling twelve-pound iron balls), which were needed to knock down the walls of the Alamo.

De la Peña accused Santa Anna of pushing forward the attack before his big guns arrived in the fear that Travis might finally surrender and rob the Mexican general of a dramatic victory. Santa Anna, he asserted, "wanted to cause a sensation and would have regretted taking the Alamo without clamor and without bloodshed." The Mexican rank and file, said de la Peña, saw the battle of the Alamo as a "defeat" because of the many men who died for the vanity of a commander who cared nothing for their lives.

The Mexican soldiers who wearily formed into decimated ranks in the immediate aftermath of the battle responded "icily" to Santa Anna's victory speech, reported de la Peña, and he claimed that this "coolness" on the part of the troops was partially the result of an "unpleasant incident" that had occurred after the end of the fighting and shortly before Santa Anna's address. De la Peña was referring to what he called the "base murder" of seven surviving defenders.

The young Mexican officer was watching as the prisoners were brought before Santa Anna by General Manuel Castrillón, who had taken the men under his protection as the battle came to an end. De la Peña noticed that "among them was one of great stature, well proportioned, with regular features, in whose face there was the imprint of adversity, but in whom one also noticed a degree of resignation and nobility that did him honor." He identified the man as David Crockett, "well known in North America for his unusual adventures."

Santa Anna responded to Castrillón's intervention on the prisoners' behalf "with a gesture of indignation" and ordered that the captives be shot on the spot. When the Mexican troops standing closest to the prisoners hesitated to carry out the rash command, officers from Santa Anna's own retinue stepped forward, wrote de la Peña, "and with swords in hand, fell upon these unfortunate, defenseless men just as a tiger leaps upon his prey." As the men were "tortured before they were killed," de la Peña "turned away horrified in order not to witness such a barbarous scene." Long after the war was over, he was haunted by the memory: "My ear can still hear the penetrating, doleful sound of the victims."

For the rest of the war, and in the remainder of his narrative, de la Peña found nothing to praise in the conduct of Santa Anna. He accused the general of providing for almost no medical corps, leading to the horrible and senseless deaths of many of the soldiers wounded in the taking of the Alamo. Santa Anna's careless delay in dispatching his troops after the battle to engage Sam Houston's army, thought de la Peña, proved how needless the premature assault on the Alamo had been. The soldiers who were at last sent eastward received inadequate rations, which he angrily attributed to both incompetence and corruption in the high command. Moreover, de la Peña believed that Santa Anna roused himself to leave the comforts of Béxar in pursuit of the remaining rebels only after word reached him of General Urrea's stunning victories in his drive up the Texas coastal plain.

As we have seen, José Urrea had on March 20 forced the surrender of Colonel James W. Fannin and several hundred of his men as they attempted to retreat from Goliad. Urrea sent the captive Texans back to the Goliad presidio, along with orders that they be well treated, but it was Santa Anna, in the meantime, who sent orders to Goliad in triplicate (and an aide to see that they were carried out) to the effect that the prisoners held there were to be immediately shot. Over General Urrea's objections, the orders were carried out.

It's not a simple matter to kill over four hundred desperate men. While the Texan wounded were left inside the presidio to meet their fate with Fannin, the rest were told that they were going to be repatriated. According to de la Peña, "they were requested to take their knapsacks to make them believe this unworthy falsehood, which they so trusted that they started singing as they began their march." As both Herman Ehrenberg and de la Peña recounted in their memoirs, the prisoners were divided into three companies, marched away from the presidio in different directions, and then suddenly shot at close range. In the ensuing chaos of smoke and screams, almost thirty of the captives, including Ehrenberg, managed to escape.

De la Peña, who interviewed a number of eyewitnesses to the executions when he passed through Goliad during the Mexican army's retreat from Texas, thought that such "cold-blooded murder" demoralized the Mexican troops and damaged their nation's cause. In his narrative of the rebellion he repeatedly contrasted the genuine successes and conciliatory actions of Urrea with the cruelty and costly vanity of Santa Anna.

The dearly-won "victory" at the Alamo would be Santa Anna's last of this war. After finally leaving San Antonio on March 31, he overtook and passed de la Peña's unit, pushing rapidly eastward in pursuit of both Sam Houston's retreating army and the politicians who had declared the independence of Texas on March 2. Houston, for his part, abandoned his line of defense on the Colorado River after receiving word of Fannin's defeat. Upon reaching the Brazos River, he eluded Santa Anna by retreating once again, barely persuading his troops, who were spoiling for a fight, to evacuate the Anglo-Texan "capital" of San Felipe de Austin. He took them north up the muddy banks of the Brazos to seek food, shelter, medicine, and a chance to regroup at the immense plantation of Jared Groce. For the next two weeks, Houston drilled, fed, and rested his remaining force of several hundred men—the Texans' last hope.

Santa Anna was prevented from crossing the Brazos at San Felipe by a few stubborn Texan riflemen on the opposite bank, left behind by Houston at their own insistence. The Mexican general chose to turn south, moving downstream until he found a safe crossing at Thompson's Ferry. He no longer considered Houston's army a threat, and his spies informed him that the rebel Texan government was just a few miles away at the little town of Harrisburg. The thought of snuffing out the rebellion by capturing its political leaders, including the apostate Mexican statesman Lorenzo de Zavala (who was now the Texan vice president), was irresistible to Santa Anna. With an advance guard of fewer than a thousand men, the commander left the bulk of his army behind on the Brazos in order to make the bold strike.

His forces missed the Texan officials by a few hours at Harrisburg and by only a few minutes as they chased them to the edge of Galveston Bay. The rowboat carrying the Texan officials to the relative safety of a ship bound for Galveston Island was still in rifle range when the Mexican cavalry galloped up to the dock at Morgan's Point, but a gallant Colonel Juan Almonte ordered his men to hold their fire since there were women in the fleeing party.

Having heard that Houston was finally on the move again, Santa Anna turned north on April 19 toward Lynch's Ferry on the San Jacinto River, where he hoped to block Houston's path to the east. Houston, having learned from a captured Mexican courier that Santa Anna had cut himself loose from the main force of the Mexican army, was rushing toward the same spot. The critical moment had come.

That a critical moment could arrive this late in the war, when few Texans had even survived—much less won—any engagement with the enemy since December, would have shocked most officers in the Mexican army. Their undefeated forces were securing the lower Brazos, one of the richest agricultural areas of Texas. General Urrea had already captured the river towns of Brazoria and Columbia and was headed toward the ocean port of Velasco. General Vicente Filisola, whom Santa Anna had left in command of the bulk of his forces, was at Thompson's Ferry.

It was in the mid-afternoon of April 22 when José Enrique de la Peña, who was with the army on the Brazos under General Filisola, noticed that troops who had been crossing to the east bank of the river all day were suddenly reversing direction and being ferried back to the west side. By five o'clock rumors were flying that Santa Anna had been surprised and defeated; by the next day the few Mexican soldiers who had escaped the disaster confirmed their massive defeat on the banks of the San Jacinto. Filisola sent urgent orders to General Urrea to join him and the other Mexican generals in an emergency council of war. They did not yet know whether Santa Anna was dead or alive.

Houston had beaten Santa Anna to Lynch's Ferry by no more than four or five hours. With most of his infantry remaining hidden in the trees along Buffalo Bayou, Houston allowed only limited cavalry skirmishing on April 20, the first day of contact. Santa Anna also delayed serious offensive action, as he expected reinforcements to reach him shortly from the Brazos. When General Cos and four hundred men arrived without interference on the morning of April 21 after marching through the night, Santa Anna thought that he had the now-outnumbered Texans exactly where he wanted them. After Houston showed no sign of an attack by mid-afternoon, the Mexican commander, who had also been up all night, decided that it was time that he and his reinforcements get some sleep. Time, Santa Anna believed, was on his side.

The naps were interrupted when Houston's desperate and bloody-minded Texans swept across the unsuspecting Mexican camp shortly after four o'clock. By nightfall, Santa Anna was a fugitive hiding in the high grass, over six hundred of his men were dead, and over seven hundred had been captured. The next day he was discovered and taken before the wounded General Houston, whose ankle had been shattered by a bullet during the Texan charge. The Mexican commander in chief soon agreed to order his remaining armies out of Texas. Santa Anna's overconfidence and carelessness had seemingly ended the war and handed the Texans their unlikely independence.

But on April 23, José Enrique de la Peña did not see it this way. He was sure that if General Filisola moved quickly against Houston, the outcome could be reversed. De la Peña was enraged when Filisola instead immediately pulled back from his position on the Brazos, and he was disappointed beyond words when his hero, General Urrea, submitted to Filisola's authority and did not insist on a continued offensive. Filisola, even before he learned of Santa Anna's fate, ordered a fallback to the Colorado River, where he could safely await further orders from his government.

The last quarter of de la Peña's narrative is the bitter story of a Mexican retreat that became a nightmare when torrential rains turned the rich Texan soil to glue. By the time the Mexicans emerged from what they called the *Mar de Lodo* (the "Sea of Mud") their Texas campaign was doomed. Much of their equipment and ordnance had been left mired in the muck. With insufficient supplies and officers who were already blaming one another for the defeat, Santa Anna's once-proud army was slouching toward Matamoros at the point when de la Peña's published diary comes to an abrupt end on June 11, 1836.

This was quite a narrative! Could a forger—*would* a forger—have created a document of such length and detail, covering not only Mexican military operations but also the rivalries and jealousies within the Mexican high command? I had my doubts. It was certainly not likely if the motive of the hoax were only to trash the reputation of Davy Crockett. Beyond my gut feeling that this manuscript was the work of an actual Mexican officer, were there any clues in Perry's English translation that might solve the mystery of the Urrea anachronism and help to establish the authenticity (or the fraudulence) of the de la Peña diary?

One such clue came from an unlikely source: the photocopies of selected pages of the de la Peña manuscripts that were included in the Texas A&M University Press edition of the diary. The final signature page of the September 15, 1836, "prologue letter" had been reproduced, and I could not help noticing a discrepancy between the original Spanish and Perry's rendering of a key sentence. The first sentence of the last paragraph of the letter begins as follows: "*Si con dar a luz mis apuntes consigo el noble objeto que me he propuesto de vindicar el honor de esta infortunada Nación y el del ejército, que acaban de ser mancillados, . . .*" Perry translated this phrase as: "If in bringing forth my notes I accomplish the noble objectives I have pursued in vindicating the honor of this unfortunate nation and its army, which recently has been tarnished, . . . "

Final page of de la Peña's letter of September 15, 1836. (COURTESY OF THE CENTER FOR AMERICAN HISTORY, UNIVERSITY OF TEXAS AT AUSTIN.)

Perry has changed de la Peña's "*noble objeto*" (which may be translated as "noble aim" or "noble goal") from singular to plural, and she has mistranslated the verb form "*me he propuesto*," which is the past participle of "*proponerse*," meaning "to plan" or "to resolve." Thus de la Peña is actually writing on September 15, 1836, not about the publication of his diary in terms of "the noble objectives I have pursued," but rather in terms of "the noble goal which I have planned," or more literally, "the noble goal which I have set for myself." De la Peña seemed to be saying that he had not yet accomplished his "noble goal."

Were there other such lapses, I wondered, that might alter our understanding of when and under what circumstances de la Peña had completed his work? I was beginning to think that I needed to see the Mexico City edition of the diary, and not just because of this error. All through Perry's English translation there were footnote references to documents and biographical material that had been published in 1955 by J. Sánchez Garza, but not included in the 1975 edition from Texas A&M. The Spanish-language version apparently included dozens of *anexos*, or appendices, which looked especially interesting. I had to see them!

Sánchez Garza's edition was a relatively rare book, unavailable in North Carolina—and most Texas libraries would not release their copies through interlibrary loan. However, my alma mater, Rice University, came through for me, and, in mid-May of 1994, I sat down to read the editor's *Preámbulo* to *La Rebelión de Texas*. Before I had finished the first page, a sentence written by Sánchez Garza bounced me out of my chair. This is what he said (in my English translation):

The manuscript, according to the wishes of the author, is entitled: *Review and Diary* [Reseña y Diario] *of the Texas Campaign*; it was not published immediately [*no se publicó luego*] due to poverty and because Filisola and later Santa Anna used all of their tricks in order to impede it; but, nearly a hundred and twenty years later, we, lovers of the truth, however it may hurt, and with great affection for history, are retrieving it from the dust of forgetfulness so that the goal for which it was written might be fulfilled.

The man who found the diary and brought it to light was saying that it had not been published at all in the nineteenth century! How could it be, then, that the supposed experts on David Crockett and José Enrique de la Peña were saying that the diary had been published in 1836? Carmen Perry had strongly suggested as much in 1975. Texan bibliographer John H. Jenkins said in 1983 that "a version of the narrative must have appeared in September, 1836, probably in a Matamoros newspaper, but no copy of any contemporary printing can now be located." Crockett biographer Paul Andrew Hutton said repeatedly in the mid-1980s that de la Peña's diary was first published in Mexico in 1836.

The apparent common source for all of these claims was no document from the Mexican past, but a statement made by Walter Lord in the sources section of his influential 1961 Alamo narrative, *A Time to Stand*. Under de la Peña's name was the following notation: "Account originally published in Matamoros, September 1836, but suppressed by authorities." Lord said that Sánchez Garza had "republished" the diary in 1955! How did he know this? There was a suspicious grammatical similarity between his statement and Sánchez Garza's, even though the meaning was opposite. I knew that Lord did not read Spanish, because his acknowledgments section began with a posthumous tribute to Dr. Carlos E. Castañeda, who, despite failing health, had worked through a hot Austin summer in the late 1950s translating "faded manuscript[s]" and "obscure Mexican books" for Lord.

Well, why not go to the source? A quick call to Manhattan information asking if they might have a listing for Walter Lord miraculously put me in touch with the Pulitzer Prize–winning author, who was eager to help me solve the mystery. A few days later, I was holding a copy of the notes Lord had made while Carlos Castañeda dictated to him the Alamo sections of Sánchez Garza's volume. At the end was this notation: "It was published in Matamoras [*sic*] on September 15, 1836, but was immediately suppressed and not republished until 120 years later."

After a long, hot day of translating, Dr. Castañeda had evidently misread a sentence in the *Preámbulo*, an error that was almost certainly prompted by the misleading "title page" dated September 15, 1836, that Sánchez Garza included in his book. I believe that Bill Groneman was exactly on target when he said that "this page seems to have been included in Sánchez Garza's book merely as a means of opening up the narrative portion of the 'diary' and separating it from the introduction." The page does not directly "purport," despite Carmen Perry's contention, to be from an 1836 printing of the diary. You may see for yourself by turning back to p. 77.

Throughout his long preamble, Sánchez Garza states again and again that de la Peña spent more than a year revising his manuscript, but was unable to publish it during his lifetime. Moreover, the *anexos* to *La Rebelión de Texas* contain several letters written by de la Peña to Mexican newspapers in 1837, making it plain that a year after the end of the rebellion he was still making plans to (someday) publish his diary.

Alas, Walter Lord's faulty bibliographical citation had sent a whole generation of historians, including Bill Groneman, off on the wrong track. De la Peña's diary itself never "purported" to be published in that year. Thus de la Peña's reference to General Urrea's *Diario* of 1838 is not an anachronism. De la Peña could have begun his diary in 1836 and still been at work on his "commentaries" in 1838.

But wait. What about that last page of the narrative, on which de la Peña signed and dated a statement to the effect that "I have concluded this narrative during the most pressing moments, a few hours before resuming the march" on September 15, 1836? Did the Sánchez Garza edition, like that of Perry, contain this unequivocal assertion? Yes, but with a subtle difference. Instead of a printed name, as in Perry's volume, there was on the last page of *La Rebelión de Texas* a facsimile of the signature of José Enrique de la Peña. It was a signature that looked very familiar. Too familiar. It was *exactly* the same signature, down to the spacing of the smallest squiggle, as the one on the photocopy of the last page of the "prologue letter"—the one included in Perry's edition. Compare the signature on p. 94 with that reproduced on p. 89.

It was impossible that precisely the same signature could have appeared on both documents. Had Sánchez Garza simply pho-

Estos son los hechos, mexicanos, juzgad vosotros por ellos y que vuestro fallo terrible anonade a los que lo hayan merecido. Los que he presenciado los he relatado fielmente y de los que no he sido testigo ocular los he rectificado con los hombres más circunspectos y veraces. Si mi modo de sentir no agrada, la franqueza con que lo hago acreditará, al menos, que soy honrado, pues digo lo que siento y lo que juzgo sin embozo y sin que me arredre el odio de los fuertes.

He concluído en los momentos más apurados y horas antes de marchar, sabiendo ya lo de San Luis.[111]

Matamoros, Tamps., a 15 de septiembre de 1836.

José Enrique de la Peña

Final page, La Rebelión de Texas, *edited by Jesús Sánchez Garza.* (Courtesy of The Center for American History, University of Texas at Austin.)

tocopied the wrong signature? I needed to know what was on the last page of the manuscript of the narrative—was there a signature there? Could I get a copy of it? These were the questions that I threw at Dora Guerra, who was at the time the curator of Special Collections at the John Peace Library at the University of Texas at San Antonio, and thus guardian of the de la Peña manuscripts.

"Well," Dora answered, "it depends on what you mean by the last page!" It became clear from our telephone conversation that the "de la Peña diary" was neither a single document nor a simple one. I was beginning to realize that I needed to go to San Antonio and look at this stuff for myself.

Around the time that I had decided to request *La Rebelión de Texas* on interlibrary loan, I knew that I was putting in more time and effort than was justified by a prospective two-page book review. But I had a hunch, similar to the one that led me down the Houston/Ehrenberg trail, that something very interesting was waiting to be uncovered. By the time I finished my conversation with Dora Guerra, I knew I was working on something significantly more ambitious than a two-page review. Fortunately, I had already planned a research trip to Austin for the end of the summer. San Antonio was now on my itinerary as well.

Before I left for Texas, however, there were a couple of minor anomalies I had to check. The first was the question of J. Sánchez Garza's given name. I had noticed that Bill Groneman referred to him as Jesús, but that the people who should know— translator Carmen Perry and bibliographer John Jenkins—had called him José. The Mexican editor used only his first initial in *La Rebelión de Texas.* I hadn't intended to spend much time tracking down the point, but when a family trip was unexpectedly cancelled, I found myself in the North Carolina State University library on a Saturday afternoon.

The detective was right and the experts were wrong. *The National Union Catalog [of] Pre-1956 Imprints*, Volume CDXLVIII, listed the name as Jesús. Score one for Groneman. But there was another, and quite unexpected, listing in this particular volume of the catalog, where I had looked under "P" for Peña. At the top of the next column was an entry for a sixteen-page pamphlet written by José Enrique de la Peña, published in Mexico City in 1839. The title, *Una Víctima del Despotismo*, was one that I was sure I had not seen anywhere before in my pursuit of the de la Peña mystery.

The *National Union Catalog* puts little codes in its entries to let the researcher know which libraries hold the book in question. Sometimes there are whole lines of codes for a book held by multiple major libraries, but in this case there was just one: "CtY." I knew this meant "Connecticut, Yale." A quick check online told me that the pamphlet was held by the Archives and Manuscripts Department of Yale's Sterling Memorial Library— a department that is closed on Saturday!

The rest of the weekend was a mixture of hell and limbo. Early Monday morning, I contacted Archives and Manuscripts at Yale and asked how soon I could have a copy of the publication. The understanding staff agreed to send it to me immediately upon receiving my check. After two overnight deliveries—my check and their photocopy—*Una Víctima del Despotismo* lay in my hands.

The pamphlet was written by de la Peña from cell number eleven of the Inquisition Prison in Mexico City, in the form of a letter to the Mexican President Anastasio Bustamante and published with the help of friends who bore the costs. The Mexican newspapers, de la Peña complained, would no longer print his letters. The little publication is a plea for mercy from an ill and dejected soldier who believes that he is being held behind bars unjustly.

De la Peña admitted that he had participated in a Federalist rebellion (led by his hero, General José Urrea) against the Centralist government in 1838. But with such uprisings a constant feature of Mexican politics, de la Peña argued that he deserved to be free. His plaintive letter bears the date of November 6, 1839. Yale's copy of this pamphlet is the only one known to exist in any library in Mexico or the United States. When I stumbled upon it in the *National Union Catalog*, it had never been cited by any historian of Texas or the Alamo.

In the middle of the pamphlet, on pages 8 and 9, I found the following statement. (The translation and emphasis are my own.)

> I know well that it is a hard thing in our country to tell the truth to men who have influence and power to do evil, but in writing about the Texas campaign, my principal object was to vindicate the honor, tarnished in it, of the nation and the army, because ignominy ought to weigh solely upon those who merit it. . . . *In good time I will expose the causes which have prevented me from publishing my diary and the observations which I have almost completed,* but I will do it in spite of my conviction that new sorrows are going to rain down upon me, [I will do it] because the noble goal which I have set for myself will give me the courage necessary to face all difficulties, and no consideration, however strong and personal it may be to me, will cause me to retreat.

So there it is. The anachronism disappears. As late as November 1839, de la Peña is still at work on the *Reseña y Diario*, which he still intends to publish.

There is yet another clue to the authenticity of the de la Peña diary hidden in this long quotation from *Una Víctima del Despotismo*. When de la Peña refers to "the noble goal which I have set for myself," he is using exactly the same language as appears in the manuscript prologue—the letter written by him on September 15, 1836. One need not be fluent in Spanish to find the matching phrases in the following passages, the first from the allegedly forged de la Peña papers, the second from the rare 1839 pamphlet:

> *Si con dar a luz mis apuntes consigo el noble objeto que me he propuesto de vindicar el honor de esta infortunada Nación y el del ejército, que acaban de ser mancillados, . . .*

> *. . . al escribir la campaña de Tejas, mi principal objeto fué vindicar el honor de la nacion y el del ejército mancillados en ella, . . . el noble objeto que me he propuesto me dará el valor necesario para arrostrar con todos los inconvenientes . . .*

Those who have argued that the de la Peña manuscripts are fraudulent have tried, unsuccessfully, to show that language used in these writings is similar to that of other, later works that have been utilized by a forger. To date, the only verbatim match of language from these papers is with the words of this little document written by de la Peña himself in a cell in a Mexico City prison. No forger could have written the "prologue letter" without having first seen *Una Víctima del Despotismo*. And then the forger would have to have kept very, very quiet about this pamphlet's existence. Of course, Sánchez Garza could have turned up a copy of *Una Víctima* in his antiques shop, and he could have found a Laflin (or a Laffite!) to do his dirty work with pen and ink. Remember that Charles Hamilton, author of *Great Forgers and Famous Fakes*, certified that Laflin was indeed the man who had forged the diary.

That was the other thing bothering me as I packed for my Texas trip. I was about to write an article-length refutation (instead of a two-page review) of Bill Groneman's forgery hypothesis, and thus go head-to-head against Hamilton—the man who in the 1980s had gained renown by exposing as a fraud a set of highly publicized "Hitler Diaries." Could he also blow away my claims of de la Peña's authenticity? I needed to know what he could tell me. Fortunately, on the photocopy of the certificate that Bill Groneman provided in *Defense of a Legend* was a tiny New York City telephone number for "Charles Hamilton, Hand-writing Expert." So I (nervously) called him up. After all, I'd had pretty good luck with Walter Lord!

Charles Hamilton was no Walter Lord. He was blowing smoke. He had never been to San Antonio, never seen the actual manuscripts. His Olympian opinion had come from examining the same photocopies in Carmen Perry's published translation that I had been looking at. And when I asked him specifically what had convinced him that John Laflin was the creator of the multiple handwritings visible on these pages, Hamilton gave me nothing but boilerplate. It was, he said, only "the eye of the ex-pert" that could see the connection between Laflin and the hand-writing on the documents in San Antonio—I would just have to trust him. I didn't, and even though he brought out a revised edition of *Great Forgers* in 1996 that includes a discussion of the de la Peña papers, I remain unconvinced. (Charles Hamilton died in 1997.)

On a scorching San Antonio summer day in 1994, Dora Guerra welcomed me to the Special Collections Department of the UTSA Library, a quiet and cool place to work, complete with both Dora's considerable expertise and multiple reference works to answer my every question. My first question, of course, was about that "last page" of de la Peña's narrative. After several days of work with the manuscripts, I found that there were indeed two versions of the diary present. The first was not the actual original, but a 109-page "clean copy" of the original, written out by de la Peña in Matamoros in the summer of 1836. The second was a narrative of more than four hundred pages, based on and incorporating the diary. It was this longer version that was published by both Jesús Sánchez Garza and Carmen Perry.

The manuscript version of this narrative abruptly breaks off with a diary entry for June 11, 1836. There is no date or signature on this final page. However, Sánchez Garza did not make up his published conclusion from whole cloth. Amid the de la Peña papers is a little booklet in which the resident of cell number eleven kept memos to himself along with bits of writing that he intended to add to the narrative during the editing process. The last item in the booklet is de la Peña's *Modelo de la conclucion.* It is also unsigned and undated. But with the omission of a single embarrassing sentence (you may guess which one) and one inconvenient qualifier, both Sánchez Garza and Perry printed the feisty de la Peña's "model conclusion" on the last page of each of their narratives, both of them also adding for good measure the September 15 date and the de la Peña signature. Here is my translation of de la Peña's conclusion:

> These are the facts, Mexicans. Judge for yourselves, and may your terrible verdict annihilate those who deserve it. The events at which I have been present I have related faithfully, and those to which I have not been an eyewitness, I have confirmed with men most circumspect and truthful. If my mode of feeling is not agreeable, the frankness with which I have worked will testify at least that I am honest, in that I say what I feel and I judge without dissembling

and without fearing the hatred of the strong. Tornel [the Minister of War] is a prick [*un carajo*], Santa Anna a very large prick [*un carajote*], and Filisola an <u>Italian.</u>

I have half finished [*He medio concluido*] in the most difficult moments, and hours before marching, knowing already about San Luis [Potosí]."

After silently passing over de la Peña's profanity, both Sánchez Garza and Perry also ignored the critical qualifier "half" [*medio*] in de la Peña's phrase, "*He medio concluido*." (Perry added the words "this narrative.") With de la Peña's task only half finished, there is still no anachronism, whether or not de la Peña wrote this sentence on September 15, 1836.

My work with these manuscripts, in 1994 and over the decade that followed, has convinced me that they are authentic, that this is indeed the narrative created by José Enrique de la Peña as he sought to explain to Mexico how Texas was lost. But just as in the case of Herman Ehrenberg's unquestionably authentic narrative of the Texas Revolution, we must go on to question de la Peña's *reliability.* Can we believe his story about how Davy Crockett died? That is the subject of the next chapter.

[Note: In 1998 the Peace family, which had maintained ownership of the manuscript of the de la Peña *Reseña y Diario* while it was on loan to UTSA, put the document up for sale at a public auction. It brought almost $400,000, enough to put it in the 2000 edition of *Guinness World Records* for "The Most Valuable Diary." The purchasers subsequently donated these papers to the Center for American History at the University of Texas at Austin, where they are available to researchers today.

After the arrival of the de la Peña manuscript in Austin, it was subjected to extensive forensic tests as well as handwriting analysis by Professor David B. Gracy II of the Graduate School of Library and Information Science at the University of Texas at Austin. His findings were published in the October 2001 issue of the *Southwestern Historical Quarterly*, along with his conclusion "that the manuscript account of the Texas campaign purported to be the product of José Enrique de la Peña written in the years following the campaign is, indeed, what it is purported to be."]

· *Three* ·

LOOKING FOR DAVY

THE MEMOIR OF LIEUTENANT COLONEL JOSÉ ENRIQUE DE LA Peña is a rich and revealing document, written by a junior officer who witnessed first-hand both the decisions made by his superiors and the effects of those decisions on ordinary soldiers. De la Peña writes movingly of the hardships suffered by the Mexican army, in the costly "victory" at the Alamo as well as in the ignominious retreat following Santa Anna's surprising defeat at San Jacinto. Infused with both patriotism and a passionate criticism of the military's high command, the "de la Peña diary" offers a fascinating perspective on the inner dynamics of the Mexican side of the Texas Revolution.

Most American commentators on de la Peña, however, focused their attention on a single paragraph in Carmen Perry's 1975 English translation. Here is the passage that caused all the ruckus:

> Some seven men had survived the general carnage [of the Battle of the Alamo] and, under the protection of General Castrillón, they were brought before Santa Anna. Among them was one of great stature, well proportioned, with regular features, in whose face

there was the imprint of adversity, but in whom one also noticed a degree of resignation and nobility that did him honor. He was the naturalist David Crockett, well known in North America for his unusual adventures, who had undertaken to explore the country and who, finding himself in Béjar at the very moment of surprise, had taken refuge in the Alamo, fearing that his status as a foreigner might not be respected. Santa Anna answered Castrillón's intervention in Crockett's behalf with a gesture of indignation and, addressing himself to the sappers, the troops closest to him, ordered his execution. The commanders and officers were outraged at this action and did not support the order, hoping that once the fury of the moment had blown over these men would be spared; but several officers who were around the president and who, perhaps, had not been present during the moment of danger, became noteworthy by an infamous deed, surpassing the soldiers in cruelty. They thrust themselves forward, in order to flatter their commander, and with swords in hand, fell upon these unfortunate, defenseless men just as a tiger leaps upon his prey. Though tortured before they were killed, these unfortunates died without complaining and without humiliating themselves before their torturers. It was rumored that General Sesma was one of them; I will not bear witness to this, for though present, I turned away horrified in order not to witness such a barbarous scene.

There were dozens of armchair zealots who weighed in against de la Peña's version of history by arguing that Davy Crockett would never have allowed himself to be captured alive. Some of the hate mail received by Perry and by Dan Kilgore (who published *How Did Davy Die?* in 1978) was especially vivid. A writer from West Anniston, Alabama, who wanted Kilgore's mouth washed out with soap (and who obviously felt a strong personal affinity for Crockett), concluded a long, rambling letter with the following declaration:

If a diagnosis is in your opinionated anatomy you may write in your memo's [*sic*] several facts concerning white-Southern men, age 17 on: Countenance is excellent, keen eyesight, healthy, and indeed will battle it out with you fists, knives, guns or will climb up on the roof of a Texas-based church [and] fight in front of God, women & everybody. . . . [B]efore I would have allowed a pompous, filthy-mouthed dog-of-a-man such as "General" Santa Ana to capture me I'd shoot myself two to three times, vitally.

Other critics, whose views of the past were more firmly grounded in the documentary record, pointed to an apparent absurdity produced by the de la Peña narrative. One of the best-known Texan eyewitness accounts of the immediate aftermath of the Alamo battle is that of a Tejano, Francisco Antonio Ruiz, the *alcalde* (or mayor) of San Antonio at the time. On the morning of March 6, Ruiz was summoned to the Alamo by Santa Anna.* The general wanted someone familiar with the defenders to accompany him on a ghastly tour through battle site, "as he was desirous to have [the bodies of] Col. Travis, Bowie, and Crockett shown to him." Those who have questioned the de la Peña diary's authenticity have argued that Santa Anna would hardly have asked for Crockett's body to be identified if only moments before he had ordered this famous man to be killed as he stood before him. That Santa Anna knew whose death he was

---

*Santa Anna was probably unaware that Ruiz's father, José Francisco Ruiz, had four days earlier (along with his nephew José Antonio Navarro) signed the Texas Declaration of Independence. These two representatives from Béxar to the Convention at Washington-on-the-Brazos were the only native Texans among the fifty-nine men who affixed their names to that document. (Lorenzo de Zavala, who became the Texas Republic's vice president after signing the declaration, was a native of Yucatán.)

dictating is indeed the impression given by Carmen Perry's translation of the critical moment: "Santa Anna answered Castrillón's intervention in Crockett's behalf with a gesture of indignation and, addressing himself to the sappers, the troops closest to him, ordered his execution."

But this is not what de la Peña wrote. The exact words in his manuscript are: "*Santa Anna contestó a la intervención de Castrillón con un gesto de indignación y dirigiéndose en seguida a los zapadores, que era la tropa que tenía más cerca, mandó que los fusilaran.*" Perry added a reference to Crockett not present in the original sentence, and also altered the last phrase from "ordered that they shoot them"—meaning that the troops should shoot Castrillón's prisoners—to say instead that Santa Anna "ordered his [i.e., Crockett's] execution."

This insertion of Crockett at the center of both Castrillón's intervention and Santa Anna's execution order led most of Perry's readers to assume falsely that the Mexican president knew the identity of the illustrious prisoner he had condemned—a conclusion not supported by the Spanish text. Translators must always make difficult decisions, and perhaps Perry was trying to be helpful to her readers by clarifying Crockett's fate amid the profusion of Spanish pronouns. But the unintended result was to alter the scene in a way that brought it into apparent contradiction with the memoir of *alcalde* Ruiz. That contradiction disappears when de la Peña's original version is consulted.

A remarkable number of critics have challenged the authenticity of the de la Peña manuscripts while ignoring the actual text of the documents in question. In the case of this crucial passage describing Santa Anna's execution order, the discrepancy between text and translation could be observed without the necessity of a trip to San Antonio to examine the manuscripts in person, or even the need to seek out the rare Mexico City edition of *La Rebelión de Texas*. The original "Davy Crockett page" of the memoir was one of several facsimiles that illustrated the 1975 Texas A&M edition of *With Santa Anna in Texas* and was thus readily available to anyone who was willing and able to decipher the Spanish script.

Other discrepancies were not so easily resolved. Shortly after I submitted my critique of *Defense of a Legend* for publication, Bill Groneman and I compared notes in a lengthy telephone conversation. I told Bill of my discovery at Yale of the 1839 de la Peña pamphlet written from prison, which had to my satisfaction disproved his charge that the diary contained a fatal anachronism. I offered him the cold comfort of the centuries-old methodological wisdom of Francis Bacon: "Truth arises more readily from error than from confusion." Groneman had performed a great service, I told him, by advancing a flawed hypothesis that pointed the way to the truth, after so many other historians had merely spread their own confusion by repeating unsubstantiated claims about the diary.

Bill returned the favor by letting me know that an even more serious anachronism had been found in the meantime, a possible "smoking gun" that might well prove his accusation of forgery. It had been discovered by Groneman's friend and fellow "doubting" historian, Thomas Ricks Lindley, a former military policeman living in Austin who has established a reputation as one of the most assiduous researchers into the documentary records of the Texas Revolution.

Tom Lindley recognized a paragraph within a footnote in the published de la Peña diaries (both the English and Spanish editions) that appeared to have been lifted *in toto* from the published memoirs of General Vicente Filisola—writings that appeared almost a decade after de la Peña's presumed death in the early 1840s. At first I tried to console myself with my own corollary to the dictum of Francis Bacon: "If it's the truth you're after, it's almost as much fun to be proven wrong as it is to be proven right." Almost, but not quite. Unready to throw in the towel, I seized upon an unexpected opportunity to return to San Antonio to see whether the manuscripts themselves were compromised by such a telltale flaw.

The "Filisola footnote" consisted of an accounting of the Mexican and Texan losses at the Alamo that contrasted the figures reported by General Santa Anna (600 Texans killed compared to only 70 Mexicans) with an official report compiled by General Juan de Andrade during the occupation of San Antonio. Andrade listed 60 Mexican officers and men killed, and Filisola added that just over 200 Texans had died.* (De la Peña himself claimed to have counted 253 Texan bodies.)

Both Perry and Mexican editor Jesús Sánchez Garza seemed to indicate that de la Peña himself was the author of the footnote containing language identical to Filisola's, but the manuscript showed otherwise. About a third of the way into his memoir, as he discussed the casualties suffered by both armies at the

---

*Perry's translation also inadvertently transposed some figures from Andrade's report, which had listed 8 Mexican officers dead and 18 wounded along with 52 Mexican soldiers dead and 233 wounded. The published English translation incorrectly reported (on page 54) these last figures as 252 dead and 33 wounded.

The "Filisola footnote" in embryo. From the de la Peña Papers, Packet II, quarto 36, page 3. (COURTESY OF THE CENTER FOR AMERICAN HISTORY, UNIVERSITY OF TEXAS AT AUSTIN.)

Alamo, de la Peña wrote this sentence: "*El siguiente estado man-ifiesta exactam.te la [pérdida] q.e tubimos (Aqui el estado).*" Or in English: "The following report shows exactly that [i.e., the loss] which we had (Here the report)." But this sentence has been scratched out in the manuscript, and the following note inserted in its place and along the side of the page: "*Veanse los documen-tos n . . . el 2.o de los cuales manifiesta exactam.te la [pérdida] q.e tubimos.*" The English translation is: "See the documents, n . . . the second of which shows exactly that [i.e., the loss] which we had." (This manuscript sheet is shown on p. 109.)

What do these textual changes show? Most plausibly, that the imprisoned de la Peña, not having the documents in question be-fore him (or even being able to recall their exact names), was writing a note to himself to the effect that this is where the doc-uments outlining the Mexican losses were to be placed in the published manuscript. At precisely this point in the text as pub-lished over a century later, in good faith if not with the best pro-fessional editorial technique, Sánchez Garza (followed closely by Perry) inserted into de la Peña's text a footnote referring to two appended documents: the 1836 reports from Generals Santa Anna and Andrade. And for good measure, though perhaps not with good judgment, Sánchez Garza (again followed by Perry) also threw into the footnote a paragraph on Texan casualties from the same part of Filisola's 1849 *Memorias para la Historia de la Guerra de Tejas* that contained Andrade's report. De la Peña's original page contains neither plagiarism nor anachronism.

I examined this page of the manuscript with considerable re-lief in October of 1994, just as my critical review of Bill Grone-man's book was being published under the title "The Little Book

That Wasn't There: The Myth and Mystery of the de la Peña Diary." (The "Little Book" in the title was the imaginary 1836 edition of the diary.)

In the years that have followed, it has sometimes seemed as if Tom Lindley, Bill Groneman, and I have been emulating the endless mutual recriminations hurled at one another by the leaders of the Mexican army in the aftermath of San Jacinto. Bill and I published five dueling essays in the academic journal *Military History of the West* in 1995 and 1996, and in the same years Tom and I debated the accuracy and authenticity of the de la Peña manuscripts through six long parry-and-thrust articles in *The Alamo Journal.*

In many cases, the attacks on de la Peña have been based on both the differences and similarities that have emerged between his memoir and those of the other Mexican officers, most notably Filisola, who offered their own post-war explanations of who lost Texas and why. In the midst of these modern debates, I have sometimes felt that de la Peña has been caught in a kind of *Catch-22* dilemma: if his narrative disagrees with another source, it falls under suspicion because its "facts" are wrong; if his narrative agrees too closely with another writer, the charge is plagiarism against the alleged "forger." In every case so far, however, each supposed "smoking gun" has itself gone up in smoke when the original sources are examined in detail.

Material evidence can also be brought to bear on de la Peña's reliability. In 1996 I received a call from an intense pediatrician in Wharton, Texas. Dr. Gregg Dimmick was the leader of a team of amateur archaeologists that also included a cattle rancher, a railroad worker, and an airplane mechanic. They were using metal detectors to dig up artifacts left behind when the Mexicans retreated across the mud flats of Wharton County, and they had run into a problem with de la Peña, whose description of the retreat they were trying to square with the facts on (or under) the ground.

As de la Peña described the efforts of the Mexican army to extract itself from the *Mar de Lodo* (the "sea of mud") he noted that the retreat turned back upon itself when the Mexicans reached a swollen river (today known as West Bernard Creek) that could not be crossed. Narrating the army's march back toward the east as it retraced its own muddy footsteps, de la Peña (as translated by Perry) wrote: "Passing by the place where we had camped on the 26th [of April], we made a 45 degree turn to the left and continued our march, crossing an immense lagoon, for the whole march has been through a swamp . . . "

The problem, said Dimmick, was that the trail of Mexican artifacts his team was extracting from the muck did not follow this forty-five-degree turn to the northeast. With commendable caution, the doctor did not immediately conclude that the de la Peña diary was a fraud, but instead called me to ask whether this passage accurately reflected the Spanish original. It did not. A quick check showed what de la Peña had written: "*dimos un cuarto de conberción por la izquierda*" ("we made a quarter turn to the left"). Not a forty-five-degree turn to the northeast, but a ninety-degree turn to the north. Perry's slip (in either geometry or translation) had sent the amateur archaeologists off on the wrong track. However, when they moved north, toward the ultimately higher ground that the Mexican officers had been seeking in order to head west again toward the Colorado River, Dimmick's team found the artifacts they were looking for.

Today the pediatrician and his colleagues are the co-authors of two technical articles on the Mexican retreat published by the Houston Archaeological Society, and they have amassed through their mucky labors the largest known collection of Mexican military artifacts from the Texas Revolution. The team and their newfound prizes were the subject of a History Channel feature in March 2001. Among the howitzer shells, epaulets, cannon balls, canister shot, and trigger guards that they have unearthed (many of which are now on loan for display at the Alamo), are a few nails found together in parallel arrangement. The only known source who mentions that the Mexican army, stuck in the mud and desperately trying to lighten their wagon loads, were throwing away not only the military items but also "*clavazón*" (sets of square nails cast in parallel rows) is de la Peña.

Gregg Dimmick has become a genuine authority on the Mexican retreat across central Texas (teaching himself to read Spanish in the process), and his recently completed scholarly analysis of the documentary and archaeological record of the crossing of the *Mar de Lodo* has been accepted for publication by the Texas State Historical Association. It is noteworthy that while comparing the many written accounts of the retreat to the archaeological evidence of the Mexicans' campsites and marching routes, he has found de la Peña's narrative to be the most accurate of the lot.

This convergence of archaeological and documentary evidence is what the nineteenth-century philosopher of science William Whewell called a "consilience of induction," or "coincidences of results drawn from distant parts of [a] subject." It is the means, quite simply put, by which we determine what it is that we believe to be true. When various lines of inquiry—forensic, archaeological, linguistic, documentary—converge toward the same conclusion, their cumulative power of persuasion is immense. When, on the other hand, different methodological approaches to a question yield opposing results, it is time to develop a new hypothesis that will better satisfy all of the available evidence.

Not all other lines of inquiry into the de la Peña narrative are as unambiguously supportive as Dimmick's archaeology. Critics such as Bill Groneman and Tom Lindley have examined the manuscripts and noted several problems with the key passage describing the death of Crockett.

Remember, first, that there are two parts to de la Peña's manuscripts: the "clean copy" of the 1836 diary and a longer second narrative, apparently composed in the three or four years following. As it happens, there is no mention whatsoever of the Alamo executions in the first de la Peña document (the 1836 diary). Only in the longer, second narrative does the Crockett story appear, and there it is found on a single two-sided page inserted between the more usual "quartos" (the four-sided folded sheets of paper favored by the creators of the manuscript). Significantly, one must say "creators" because, as the critics have pointed out, the handwriting in the de la Peña manuscript clearly changes from time to time within the second "memoir" portion of the papers, where at least four different hands can be distinguished. The handwriting changes, moreover, just as the Crockett tale begins.

It should be noted that in 2002 Tom Lindley made public his revised opinion that the "diary" portion of the de la Peña papers is authentic. He based his conclusion on a comparison of the manuscript with samples of José Enrique de la Peña's handwriting found in Mexican military and judicial records. But because of the aggregation of different handwritings in the longer memoir (as well as other problems with its contents), Lindley continues to denounce the second section of the manuscripts as a fake.

The multiple handwritings in the de la Peña papers, which are noticeable even in the few pages of the original that were reproduced in Carmen Perry's published translation, raise interesting and at first baffling questions. Would a skillful forger use four or more different handwriting styles in crafting a hoax as elaborate as this is alleged to be? How could de la Peña himself, working alone, have produced such a motley document?

To answer this conundrum, we must understand de la Peña's personal circumstances as he worked on his memoir between 1837 and 1839. One of the letters that he sent during this period is from Guadalajara, dated June 11, 1838. Today the letter may be found at the Benson Latin American Collection at the University of Texas at Austin, among the papers of the prominent Mexican politician Don Valentín Gomez Farías. The letter is in a handwriting markedly different from those visible in the diary or narrative manuscripts. Could this be proof that the "real" de la Peña had nothing at all to do with these manuscripts? Not at all: the letter states that de la Peña is so physically ill in prison that he cannot write for himself. He has been forced to use an amanuensis, and neither the body of the letter nor the signature is from his own hand.

De la Peña laments his ill health repeatedly during the years of his imprisonment—both in his published letters to the newspaper *El Cosmopolita* in Mexico City and in his pamphlet *Una Víctima del Despotismo*. Thus it is hardly surprising that he would need help in producing a narrative of over four hundred handwritten pages. Neither the change in handwriting nor the inserted sheet of paper markedly differentiates the Crockett passage from other parts of the memoir. In fact, one of the most convincing aspects of the de la Peña papers is the evidence that the narrative is very much an arrested "work-in-progress" that adverse circumstances never permitted the author to finish.

It was only in 1995, during my second summer visit to Special Collections at the University of Texas at San Antonio, that I realized just how "unfinished" the narrative was. While comparing entries for specific dates in the "clean copy" of the diary and the larger memoir, I discovered that a week of entries for June 12 through June 18 was missing from the memoir. These entries in the diary covered de la Peña's difficult journey with the Mexican army across the near-deserted territory between the Nueces and the Río Grande. These anguished commentaries detailed the hardships endured by the starving troops during their final week of retreat. The entries were overlooked by Perry and Sánchez Garza alike, who both apparently failed to realize that the "short" version of the narrative actually contained more daily entries than the longer one.

On another return trip to San Antonio the following summer, I found a little booklet of footnote texts that matched the mysterious numerals scattered by de la Peña throughout the body of his shorter "copied" diary. Each numbered note had been carefully crossed out except for the last two—and these matched the two numerals found in the final "missing week" of daily entries—the portion of the diary that de la Peña never had the chance to rewrite. All but these two entries in the notebook had been incorporated into the observations recorded in his longer, edited narrative. The booklet of crossed-out notes thus forms a kind of organic link between the two versions of the narrative, strongly suggesting that the "memoir" is every bit as authentic as the "diary" that Tom Lindley now accepts as genuine.

Reading through the remaining scraps of de la Peña's determined efforts to tell his story, I found several more booklets, some crudely made in the prison cell with torn and folded paper. One held the *Modelo de la conclucion* (described in the previous chapter) that editor Jesús Sánchez Garza employed to bring closure to de la Peña's "unfinished" narrative. Another booklet bore the title "Important additions to the diary for organizing the editing of it." On its first page, in a hasty scrawl to himself, de la Peña had written: " . . . *es importante huir de . . . [parcialidad] si quiere uno ser creido. Mucho cuid.º para que es muy dificil ser historiador.*" The handwriting was so poor—spread out in a nearly flat horizontal line across the page—that it took me several minutes to tease out the last word, which the writer had hyphenated from one line to another. I felt goose bumps on my arm when I realized what he was saying: " . . . it is important to avoid partiality if one wants to be believed. Be very careful because it is very difficult to be a historian."

I felt at this instant a flash of recognition as well as admiration—recognition of a fellow historian working to preserve and convey the truth as best he could determine it, and doing so while he was ill, imprisoned, and without the means to publish the history that he believed every Mexican should read. Because of moments like these, when I could sense the man behind the words on the page, it is difficult for me to believe that either an obsessive or a merely mercenary forger had created these rich and complex manuscripts. These papers are imbued with the messiness of real life, reflecting de la Peña's fierce struggle to complete his *Reseña y Diario*. And yet, ironically, it is this authentic strength of the papers that is also their greatest weakness. De la Peña depended upon others, not only to assist him with the physical act of writing but also to provide him with the additional material that helped to quadruple the size of his work. These additions can detract from both the immediacy and the integrity of his own eyewitness narrative.

This problem is evident, for instance, in de la Peña's descriptions of the Alamo's defenders, both those who died in combat and those who were executed. Colonel William Barret Travis, he relates, was a handsome blond who bravely traded shots with Mexican soldiers in the open plaza of the Alamo after the walls had been scaled—a scenario very much at odds with other accounts of both the way Travis appeared and the way he died. There is good evidence that the Alamo's commander was killed on the north wall of the fortress in the first minutes of the assault, with a single bullet to his forehead.

De la Peña would not have been able to recognize either Travis or Crockett on sight, and he gives no indication in his manuscript of who identified these men for him or who informed him of Crockett's alleged "alibi"—the claim that he was an innocent visitor who had taken refuge in the Alamo "at the very moment of surprise . . . fearing that his status as a foreigner might not be respected." This is certainly unlike the Crockett described by William Barret Travis, who declared in a letter to Sam Houston written from the besieged Alamo on February 25 that "the Hon[orable] David Crockett was seen at all points, animating the men to do their duty."

De la Peña's description of Crockett's last moments has been taken by some writers (most notably Jeff Long in his iconoclastic 1990 book, *Duel of Eagles*) as proof that Crockett "quit," and then "lied" and "dodged" in his efforts to save himself. This may not seem to be in character for a man who had stood up to the president of the United States: Crockett had famously clashed with Andrew Jackson over the latter's unfair treatment of the Indians, and bolted the Democratic Party for the Whig opposition. Yet it is not impossible that David Crockett was enough of a champion storyteller (and "sly politician") to attempt to talk his way out of a serious jam.

De la Peña's description of Crockett's "alibi" has nevertheless given doubters their best argument for plagiarism and fraud. The only other account suggesting that Crockett pled for his life using such an alibi was supposedly told to George Patrick, a veteran of Sam Houston's army. Following the Battle of San Jacinto, Patrick had asked the captured Mexican General Martín Perfecto de Cos how Crockett died. "When we thought that all the defenders were slain," reported Cos, he had found a well-dressed man locked in one of the rooms of the barracks. When Cos asked who he was, the man is said to have replied:

I am David Crockett, a citizen of the State of Tennessee and representative of a district of that State in the United States Congress. I have come to Texas on a visit of exploration; purposing, if permitted, to become a loyal citizen of the Republic of Mexico. I extended my visit to San Antonio, and called in the Alamo to become acquainted with the officers, and learn of them what I could of the condition of affairs. Soon after my arrival, the fort was invested by government troops, whereby I have been prevented from leaving it. And here I am yet, a noncombatant and foreigner, having taken no part in the fighting.

Cos said that he took the man to Santa Anna, repeated the man's story, and requested his release. Cos continued:

Santa Anna heard me through, but impatiently. Then he replied sharply, "You know your orders"; turned his back upon us and walked away. But, as he turned, Crockett drew from his bosom a dagger, with which he smote at him with a thrust, which if not arrested, would surely have killed him; but was met by a bayonet-thrust by the hand of a soldier through the heart; he fell and soon expired.

Obviously, Cos's alleged account of Crockett's alibi, though much more detailed, sounds similar to de la Peña's brief mention of Crockett's claim to be protected by his "status as a foreigner." But Cos's account did not come to public notice until 1939, when the Texas Folklore Society published a letter about George Patrick's conversation with the Mexican general. In truth this was not even Patrick's own letter, but that of *another* veteran of the revolution, William P. Zuber, who in 1904 had recalled Patrick's telling *him* Cos's story of the captured Crockett. Zuber said that he believed Patrick, but thought that the story told by Cos was "a gross falsehood."

Tom Lindley has argued that Zuber—not Cos or Patrick—likely fabricated the story, given his "reputation for telling Alamo tall tales." Lindley goes on to assert that if we accept that de la Peña's description of Crockett as a noncombatant "has no basis in truth or honest error, then the only explanation for it being in the de la Peña account is that the creator of the de la Peña description obtained the element from the Cos account"—an account not published until 1939.

De la Peña's account and Zuber's do indeed contain elements that are tantalizingly similar, but is twentieth-century plagiarism the only explanation for the similarities? Lindley is asking us to believe that it is possible for Zuber to make up stories, but that no one else is capable of this—not de la Peña, nor anyone who gave information to de la Peña. Lindley is also telling us that it is not just unlikely, but downright impossible, for Crockett to have made such excuses to Castrillón, to Cos, or to anyone else in the last desperate moments of his life. Note that Lindley begs the question by simply assuming that Crockett did not make such a statement: as he puts it, there can be no basis for de la Peña's story in either "truth or honest error."

Lindley also dismisses too hastily the possibility that both Zuber and Patrick could be telling the truth. Indeed, Cos might very well have told such a story to George Patrick in 1836, because after San Jacinto the captive Mexican general was in hot water with the Texans. They were accusing him of having violated the parole under which he and his surviving men had been allowed to leave Texas following his surrender at Béxar in December 1835. It would have been very much in Cos's interest to disassociate himself from Crockett's death and the Alamo executions in a way that would portray himself (instead of General Castrillón, who had died at San Jacinto) as the would-be savior and Crockett as a brave and tragic hero.

We simply do not know where de la Peña obtained his version of Crockett's unsuccessful Alamo alibi. But we do know that he spent three years in the wake of the Texas campaign reworking and expanding his diary, gathering material from multiple sources along the way. Even if the revised diary should prove to be tainted by these sources, it would remain a valuable window into the inner workings of the Mexican army. Moreover, we are fortunate that the "clean copy" of the original diary is intact, so that we may assess what has been added in de la Peña's editing process.

If de la Peña's memoir should repeat an unlikely story about Crockett, even a totally false one, this would not mean that the manuscript is not authentic. But as to *reliability*, the fact that de la Peña fashioned his longer narrative from multiple sources should make us cautious about accepting it as an authoritative account of how Davy died. Without corroboration from more reliable and immediate sources, de la Peña's story of the Alamo executions would have limited credibility.

For a basic description of the executions following the Battle of the Alamo, we do have a very credible eyewitness—one accepted even by Lindley and Groneman. Ramón Martínez Caro was a Mexican civilian who served as Santa Anna's personal secretary during the Texas campaign. In a memoir published in Mexico City in 1837, Caro was blunt in his criticism of his former boss's behavior after the battle:

Among the 183 killed there were five who were discovered by General Castrillón hiding after the assault. He took them immediately to the presence of His Excellency who had come up by this time. When he presented the prisoners he was severely reprimanded for not having killed them on the spot, after which [Santa Anna] turned his back upon Castrillón while the soldiers stepped out of their ranks and set upon the prisoners until they were killed. . . . We all witnessed this outrage which humanity condemns but which was committed as described. This is a cruel truth, but I cannot omit it.

Caro, of course, said nothing about Crockett. Moreover, the ready availability of Caro's published memoir in Mexico as de la Peña was revising his diary means that these two cannot be taken as wholly independent sources. De la Peña could have easily lifted the story of General Castrillón and his prisoners from Santa Anna's secretary. Could de la Peña have borrowed and inserted the Crockett execution story as well? Certainly. As we have seen, newspaper accounts alleging the murder of the captive Crockett were circulating in the United States by the summer of 1836.

Walter Lord found that fragmentary information (or rumors) had reached New Orleans as early as March 27—only three weeks after the battle—claiming that Crockett and a few other men had tried to surrender "but were told there was no mercy for them." However, one of the fullest and most widely circulated of the accounts of Crockett's death, and one that closely matches the scene described by Caro and de la Peña, was in a letter written to the New York *Courier and Enquirer* from Galveston Bay on June 9, 1836, "from a gentleman who has been in familiar con-

SLEUTHING THE ALAMO

versation with the Mexican prisoners there." Here is how this anonymous "gentleman" related the story "detailed by an *eye witness*":

> After the Mexicans had got possession of the Alamo, the fighting had ceased, and it was clear day light, six Americans were discovered near the wall yet unconquered, and who were instantly surrounded and ordered by General Castrillon to surrender, and who did so under a promise of his protection, finding resistance any longer in vain—indeed, perfect madness—Castrillon was brave and not cruel, and disposed to save them. He marched them up to that part of the fort where stood "his Excellency," surrounded by his murderous crew, his sycophantic officers. David Crockett was one of the six. The steady, fearless step, and undaunted tread, together with the bold demeanor of this hardy veteran—"his firmness and noble bearing," to give the words of the narrator, had a most powerful effect on himself and Castrillon. Nothing daunted he marched up boldly in front of Santa Anna, looked him steadfastly in the face, while Castrillon addressed "his Excellency"—"Sir, here are six prisoners I have taken alive; how shall I dispose of them?" Santa Anna looked at Castrillon fiercely, flew into a most violent rage, and replied, "Have I not told you before how to dispose of them? Why do you bring them to me?" At the same time his brave officers drew and plunged their swords into the bosoms of their defenceless prisoners!! So anxious and intent were these blood thirsty cowards to gratify the malignity of this inveterate tyrant, that Castrillon barely escaped being run through in the scuffle himself.

There were many more details concerning the battles of the Alamo and San Jacinto in this very long letter, including the claim that three additional wounded prisoners had been discovered in the Alamo and ordered to be instantly shot by Santa Anna. If this anonymous letter were the only corroboration of Caro's account of the killings, it might be argued (indeed it has been argued by Tom Lindley and Bill Groneman) that it was the product of an imaginative New York reporter on assignment in Texas, trying to sell more newspapers by adding the celebrity appeal of Crockett to the already widespread rumors of executions at the Alamo.

But there is more. Another letter describing an eyewitness account from a Mexican prisoner of war was written on July 19, 1836, not by a reporter but by George M. Dolson, a bilingual Texan sergeant whose letter from Texas to his brother in Michigan was published the following September in the Detroit *Democratic Free Press*. Dolson was serving as an interpreter at Camp Travis, where most of the Mexican prisoners of war were being kept on Galveston Island after the Texan victory at San Jacinto. On July 18 he had been summoned by Colonel James Morgan, the camp commander, to take down an oral deposition from one of "Santa Anna's officers." This is how Sergeant Dolson described the prisoner's story in the long letter that he wrote to his brother the following day:

He [the Mexican officer] states that on the morning the Alamo was captured, between the hours of five and six o'clock, General Castrillon, who fell at the battle of San Jacinto, entered the back room of the Alamo, and there found Crockett and five other Americans, who had defended it until defence was useless; they appeared very much agitated when the Mexican soldiers undertook to rush in after their General, but the humane General ordered his men to keep out, and, placing his hand on one breast, said, "here is a hand and a heart to protect you; come with me to the General-in-Chief, and you shall be saved." Such redeeming traits, while they ennoble in our estimation this worthy officer, yet serve to show in a more heinous light the damning atrocities of the chief. The brave but unfortunate men were marched to the tent of Santa Anna. Colonel Crockett was in the rear, had his arms folded, and appeared bold as the lion as he passed my informant (Almonte.) Santa Anna's interpreter knew Colonel Crockett, and said to my informant, "the one behind is the famous Crockett." When brought in the presence of Santa Anna, Castrillon said to him, "Santa Anna, the august, I deliver up to you six brave prisoners of war." Santa Anna replied, "who has given you orders to take prisoners, I do not want to see those men living—shoot them." As the monster uttered these words each officer turned his face the other way, and the hellhounds of the tyrant despatched the six in his presence, and within six feet of his person.

In *Defense of a Legend*, Bill Groneman argued that "there is enough nonsense in . . . [the Dolson Letter] to eliminate it as a credible source." It is, of course, not a perfect source—few ever are. No copy has ever been found of the officer's deposition. It is always possible that leading questions could have been asked, suggesting to the prisoner that Colonel Morgan was looking for evidence against Santa Anna for a possible trial for war crimes. But a family letter from a soldier in Dolson's position would have to be nonsensical indeed for us to simply throw it out of the historical court of inquiry! What is the "nonsense" that Groneman found in this document? The first is the identification of "Almonte" as the source of the story, based on the reference to "my informant (Almonte.)"

Was Dolson's "informant" Colonel Juan N. Almonte? That's what Rice University graduate student Thomas Lawrence Connelly took for granted when he stumbled across the Dolson letter in the Detroit newspaper. Connelly provided a bit of biographical material on Almonte when he published the letter in the prestigious *Journal of Southern History* in 1960, but nothing in this material placed Almonte at the scene of the interview. That would have been impossible—because Bill Groneman's claim that Almonte could not have been the informant is absolutely correct. Historians have been able to pinpoint Almonte's location in Texas from April 1836, when he was captured at San Jacinto, to late November of 1836, when he left Texas. Almonte was never held as a prisoner in Camp Travis, and certainly not on July 18, when the interview with Dolson's informant took place.

But even a cursory glance at Juan Almonte's biography should have made Connelly realize that Almonte could not have been the informant. The urbane colonel, reputedly the illegitimate son of the Mexican revolutionary hero José María Morelos, had been sent for his education to New Orleans, where he became fluent in French and English as well as his native Spanish. Moreover, Almonte's fluency in English was well known in Texas and the United States in 1836. He had spent much of the year 1834 on an inspection tour of Texas, and served for most of the following year in New York and Washington as a special representative of the Mexican government. If Almonte had been the "informant," he would not have needed Dolson as an interpreter.

So how could George Dolson have written such "nonsense"? The answer becomes clearer when we ask what Almonte was actually doing in Texas in July 1836, when Dolson wrote his letter. The Colonel was being kept as a prisoner of war with Santa Anna, Ramón Martínez Caro, and another senior Mexican officer at a heavily guarded plantation house on the Texas mainland. Almonte was serving there as Santa Anna's interpreter.

We also know from Almonte's correspondence with the Mexican government that he was familiar with the American politician and celebrity David Crockett as early as 1834, and almost certainly had seen Crockett's widely published portraits by 1836, even if he had not met him face-to-face. It's useful to remember that in Spanish, the verb "*conocer*" is used both to say that you personally "know" someone and to convey the idea that you are merely "familiar with" a personage. Dolson's informant was speaking Spanish, not English, when he said that Santa Anna's interpreter "knew"—or was familiar with—Crockett.

Finally, keep in mind that the Dolson Letter was published in a newspaper after it had been originally written out in longhand. If, as seems reasonable, Dolson realized only after writing the sentences quoted here that he had failed to identify Santa Anna's interpreter, he could have written Almonte's name in parentheses between the lines, just above its proper place in the letter. It would take only a very slight error on the part of the newspaper's typesetter to drop the name onto the wrong side of the period. When the name is placed on the other side, here is how Dolson's letter would read: Crockett "appeared bold as the lion as he passed my informant. Almonte, Santa Anna's interpreter, knew Crockett and said to my informant, 'the one behind is the famous Crockett.'" Dolson's "nonsense," in other words, can be attributed to a simple typographical error.

But Bill Groneman also points to another sentence from the Dolson Letter: "The brave but unfortunate men were marched to the tent of Santa Anna." This, he argues, produces another absurdity. Either Crockett and the prisoners were marched outside the walls of the Alamo to Santa Anna's tent, or else Santa

Anna had just set up a tent inside the walls, even before the dead had been removed from the fort. The second scenario is ludicrous, the first is demonstrably false. Several witnesses who saw Crockett's inanimate body on the morning of March 6 reported that it was lying *inside* the walls of the Alamo. How could George Dolson have written such nonsense? How could his informant, if he had truly been at the scene of Crockett's death, have said such a ridiculous thing?

He didn't. One thing we know just as surely as we can know anything in history is that Dolson's informant did *not* say the words: "The brave but unfortunate men were marched to the tent of Santa Anna." He couldn't have said it in just this way because he didn't speak English. He said something in Spanish that George Dolson translated as these words, and Dolson, who had not arrived in Texas until after the battle of San Jacinto, was unfamiliar with the details of the Alamo and its fall. Dolson would not have realized the incongruity of the reference to Santa Anna's tent.

What might the informant have said? It must have been something that a fluent Spanish-speaker like Dolson could have interpreted as "tent." Could Dolson have mistaken some other word for "*tienda*" (the literal Spanish for "tent")? How about "*teniente*"? Could the men have been marched to Santa Anna's "lieutenant, deputy, or substitute"? Not likely. The context makes it clear that they were brought directly to the commander in chief. I believe that the similarity to "tent" was not in the *sound* of the word spoken by the informant, but in its *meaning*, that is to say, in one of its many meanings. The versatile Spanish word "*pabellón*" can mean many things: pavilion, field-bed, bell tent,

tent-like curtain, dais, bed canopy, summerhouse, national flag, bell of a wind instrument, stack of arms, or the external ear (among other things)!

If General Castrillón wanted to take his prisoners directly to Santa Anna in the immediate aftermath of the battle, as the commander in chief was striding into the Alamo, would he not march the men "to the flag of Santa Anna"? His excellency had entered the fallen fortress with a retinue, which under battlefield conditions would almost certainly have included a flag-bearer. And not just any flag. In Spanish, ordinary flags are usually called "*banderas*," but the official national flag displaying the "shield-of-arms" of governmental authority is called the "*pabellón*." Dolson's letter makes perfect sense if his informant meant that the men were marched "to the flag of Santa Anna" ("*al pabellón de Santa Anna*"). The second alleged piece of "nonsense" in Dolson's letter is most likely an innocent error of translation. The informant said "*pabellón*," meaning "flag," but Dolson heard "*pabellón*" and assumed it meant "tent."

Documents such as the Dolson Letter, which at first seem nonsensical or impenetrable, can, with greater contextual knowledge and the exercise of an informed historical imagination, be made to reveal some of their secrets. It is well to remember that with any historical document there is always a "text behind the text"—even if it consists only of the assumptions in the mind of the text's creator. In the Dolson case, however, there are quite literally "texts behind the text," with the longhand letter behind the newsprint, and the oral interview behind the letter.

What is most striking about the July 19 letter from Dolson and the earlier one written from Galveston Bay on June 9 is *not* their obvious similarities, although they are close enough in tone and content to suggest that they are likely the result of separate interviews with the same Mexican prisoner of war. Even more impressive is the compatibility of both of these descriptions of the Alamo executions with the memoir published a year *later* in Mexico City by Ramón Martínez Caro. The congruence is not perfect. Caro said five men were executed in the group, the Galveston letters each said six. (De la Peña and many of the early reports from the Alamo spoke of seven.) Caro, of course, covered the scene quickly in his book and gave few details and no names. But these very similar stories of the hapless Castrillón and his doomed prisoners could not have been produced by coincidence. What is most likely is that tellers of these tales witnessed the same tragic event.

The discrepancy in the numbers—five, six, or seven victims—seems not unreasonable for people recalling a scene weeks or months after they've witnessed it. With such written historical evidence, as with the tossing of horseshoes or hand grenades, "close" is sometimes good enough. A *perfect* match of alleged facts from disparate sources or different eyewitnesses to an event should not be the required standard of historical truth, but should instead alert the researcher to the probability of fraud. Some documents really *are* too good to be true. As humans, our perception of events, our fallible memories, and the historical evidence they produce are all rather messy commodities that do not come in perfectly wrapped packages.

Given the fragmentary and imperfect nature of historical evidence, it is of course possible to develop alternative, if implausible, scenarios. Tom Lindley has theorized that George M. Dolson appropriated the basic story of Crockett's death from the earlier Galveston letter of June 9, 1836. Dolson, believes Lindley, arranged for his own version of Crockett's murder to be published in order to ingratiate himself with his commanding officer, a Texan general named Thomas Jefferson Green, who was eager to see Santa Anna hanged. Lindley argues in turn that the earlier letter describing the same scene had been concocted with the Crockett angle added to sell newspapers. Because of the similarity of both letters to the story told by Caro in 1837, Lindley claims that Caro must have spread his version of the Alamo executions when he was in Texas, though Lindley can offer absolutely no evidence for this assertion other than its necessity for the viability of his tenuous thesis.

In a similar vein, historian William C. Davis, author of *Three Roads to the Alamo* and *Lone Star Rising*, has speculated that Caro could have stolen the story from American or Mexican newspapers that had reprinted either or both of the Galveston letters. But why would Caro, who was writing in Mexico City for an audience that would have included other eyewitnesses to the events that he described, risk his credibility by aping an American account of executions in the Alamo if he knew it to be bogus?

Of course, if Davis and Lindley are *both* right, then all of these sources must have stolen the story from each other! The theoretical scenarios of Lindley and Davis appear to be strenuous efforts to avoid the far more likely possibility that both Ramón Martínez Caro and Dolson's informant were truthful witnesses to the same bloody event at the Alamo: the execution of David Crockett and a handful of other prisoners immediately after the battle.

For all their strained logic and misplaced faith in faulty translations, most of the the the efforts of Bill Groneman and Tom Lindley to uphold the Crockett legend have at least been thoughtful
and informed by the evidence. That's more than can be said for
some of the barbs that have come my way since I entered the
fray in 1994 with my defense of de la Peña. When my first critique of Groneman's forgery hypothesis appeared, I was warned
by Kevin R. Young, "Well, you've really stepped in it now!" As
an historical interpreter who had long worked in the contentious
venues of both the Alamo and the Goliad presidio, Kevin knew
what he was talking about when it came to controversies about
the Texan past.

First, my telephone started ringing, mostly with media types
from both sides of the Atlantic looking for a sound bite (which
I wasn't going to give them) to the effect that "Crockett was a
coward!" Then I started receiving my own hate mail. A brief article outlining the fruits of my detective work in *Sallyport* (the
magazine of Rice University) produced this accusatory response
from an irate alumnus:

> . . . how can you be sure that José Enrique de la Peña was not hid-
> ing behind a pile of rubble until the 1836 action at the Alamo had
> ceased then capitalized on his spare time while languishing in a
> Mexican prison by writing fiction on a popular subject of the times,
> the Texas Revolution?
>
> Indeed, there appears to be a considerable similarity of motives
> between de la Peña and Crisp, i.e., inventing, writing, and market-
> ing a contrarian neohistory to suit their self-interests.

This critic went on to suggest that his efforts and mine were actually part of a larger battle about the meaning of the past:

Just as the American people have elected [in 1994] a current congress that is well on the way to correct[ing] the excesses of the last forty years of political liberalism, so they are justly rebelling against legitimization and glorification of the murderous scoundrels of American history, be they Indians, Mexicans, or Japanese, at the expense of our traditional, completely documented, red-blooded, heroic Anglo ancestors.

Such attacks notwithstanding, there was also a happier sense in which Kevin Young's prediction was on target. I had also stepped directly into a strange and fascinating world of Alamo enthusiasts (and protesters) of every stripe: re-enactors, webmasters, movie buffs, kitsch collectors, political activists, military history fanatics, descendants of the actual Alamo defenders (both Anglo and Tejano), and connoisseurs of every variety of material culture associated with the Alamo—both the building and the battle—from architecture and artillery to the buttons and stitching of uniforms. Moreover, this was not a closed world. I found the level of popular interest in the Alamo as a significant piece of American history to be extraordinarily high, now made even more so with the renewed Crockett controversy, the fresh documentary discoveries, and the revived notoriety of the de la Peña diary.

Yet an undercurrent of tension remained. When Bill Groneman and I offered our conflicting verdicts on Crockett and de la Peña in March 1995 to gatherings of the Texas State Historical Association and the Alamo Battlefield Association in San Antonio, there were morbid jokes about my need for a bulletproof vest. On the Sunday following our speeches, a woman who recognized me from the previous day's events turned toward me as I walked past the Alamo. She blurted out, "I know who you are—and if I had my Bowie knife I'd gut you right now, because hanging would be too good for you!" I managed to deflect this woman's half-serious anger by engaging her in a discussion of the documentary evidence (she's since become a friend), but her passion as a self-described "Crockett loyalist" was indicative of the strong feelings that still enveloped popular memories of this long-ago battle.

De la Peña's version of events was featured in both History Channel and Discovery Channel presentations on the Alamo that aired in 1996, and in January 1997 the BBC sent a team to Texas to record a program for the radio series "Document"—the first time the series had focused on an historical document originating beyond the British Isles. Although the subject was ostensibly the de la Peña diary, the final edit of the forty-minute BBC documentary was mostly devoted to contrasting the dissenters and defenders of the traditional heroic story of Davy's death. Tom Lindley and I rehashed our arguments without shedding much new light on the subject, but there was one interview recorded by the British that stuck in my mind.

While I was with them in Austin, the BBC producers arranged a meeting at the Texas State Capitol with Andrés Tijerina, a leading Tejano historian. To my surprise (after all, this was a *radio* documentary), much of Tijerina's discussion centered on Texan historical art, and especially on the giant painting of the battle for the Alamo that hangs in the Senate Chamber of the Capitol. I remember Andrés pointing out the noble, white-shirted Crockett figure in artist Henry A. McArdle's dark and violent work, *Dawn at the Alamo*. About to be overwhelmed by a sea of dusky, demonic Mexicans (perhaps some of those "murderous scoundrels of American history"), Davy stands out in bright and heroic contrast, an icon within an icon. How, the British commentator asked during the broadcast on March 6, 1997, could de la Peña's words possibly compete in the public mind with such powerful mythic imagery?

Mythic imagery was certainly the goal of Michael Lind's *The Alamo: An Epic*, a 274-page poem in the Homeric tradition that was published on the same Alamo anniversary day as the BBC broadcast. I had to be in Austin on March 6 when Lind (then a staff writer at *The New Yorker*) was signing copies of his epic in San Antonio, but three days later our paths figuratively crossed in the pages of the *New York Times Book Review* when historian and critic Garry Wills explicitly cited my work on the de la Peña diary as he dismissed Lind's poetic defense of the Crockett legend. "Things not worth doing can sometimes be done well," said Wills, "[b]ut here is something not worth doing that is done ill . . . " He faulted Lind for accepting uncritically too many of the Alamo myths (including Crockett's heroic death in combat), despite the author's claim that he had "used plausibility, not dramatic value, as the criterion" for "choosing between varying accounts of what happened at the Alamo." Wills castigated Lind for accepting Bill Groneman's "desperate claim of forgery, though it has been definitively refuted by James Crisp" in the pages of the *Southwestern Historical Quarterly*.

This was heady stuff. I learned of the review as I was driving from Austin to San Antonio, when one of my North Carolina colleagues rang my cell phone to ask me if I knew that I was in that morning's *New York Times*. When a few days later CBS News anchor Dan Rather jumped to the defense of his fellow transplanted Texan Michael Lind in a long letter to the *Book Review* (denouncing the credibility of "testimony from a Mexican Army officer" but obviously having never read de la Peña's narrative), I couldn't help recalling what de la Peña himself had said in 1837 when he decided to intervene in the flurry of finger-pointing among the Mexican generals who were blaming each other for losing Texas: "I am a pygmy who is going into combat against giants; but, having reason on my side, I expect to come out victorious . . . " Perhaps I did share some of de la Peña's motives, after all!

That irate Rice alumnus was certainly right about one thing: whether I liked it or not (and whatever my actual motives), I was in the midst of a larger battle. And my hate mail was telling me that something sinister was involved in at least some people's ardent defense of the traditional Crockett story. I felt sure that the stubborn old issue of race was bound up with questions of myth and collective identity in the story of the Alamo and Davy's death. What I did not yet understand was why, as a historian who claimed, in essence, that the Mexicans had cruelly murdered Davy Crockett in 1836, I should be on the receiving end of hostile reactions that were laced with overtones of anti-Mexican racism.

Was there any logical (or psychological) connection between a defense of the traditional story of Davy's death in combat and a racial loathing of Mexicans? My attempts to answer this question over the next two years followed a twisted trail from the archived hate mail of the late Dan Kilgore to the canvasses of artists such as Henry A. McArdle, whose dark visions of Mexicans portrayed an enemy to whom no civilized man would ever surrender. And it was in the midst of these paintings of an imagined Texan past that I stumbled across another mystery—involving a sharp blade, a slit canvas, and an Alamo story that had lain hidden for nearly a century.

· *Four* ·

The Paintbrush
and the Knife

ON Friday, April 28, 1978, the (London) *Daily Mail* announced that an obscure Texan accountant and amateur historian by the name of Dan Kilgore "could become America's most hated man." Was Dan Kilgore a terrorist bomber? Had he taken an ax to his wife and children? No, according to the *Daily Mail*, Kilgore had "murder[ed] a myth." He had "struck a shattering blow at the Alamo legend by saying that Davy Crockett did not go down fighting." Indeed, by the time that this story appeared in London, Kilgore was already receiving "hate mail" in response to the book that he had published only the previous week: *How Did Davy Die?*

On a balmy Gulf Coast day twenty years later, in the summer of 1998, I was reading that mail in the Dan E. Kilgore Collection at the Corpus Christi campus of Texas A&M University. I was in Corpus Christi on yet another hunch, but it was a hunch born of frustration and confusion. To be honest, I was trying to understand my own hate mail.

Yes, my critics were unhappy with the way I had treated Davy. But beyond that, the letters betrayed enough anti-Mexican sentiment to convince me that there was a link, somehow, between the racial views of their authors and their emotional commitment to the heroic image of Crockett's last stand. On the face of it, though, such a link seemed illogical. Why would someone who disliked Mexicans attack me for arguing that Mexicans had murdered Crockett in cold blood? What was the connection between such prejudices and a passionate defense of the traditional narrative of Crockett's heroic death?

I had assumed that the connection would be revealed in the popular media that had shaped so many people's images of the Alamo and its meaning—the films starring Fess Parker and John Wayne being my foremost suspects. But when I went to view those movies for the first time since I was a child, I did not find what I had anticipated. These were definitely *not* the modern cinematic equivalents of the old *Texas History Movies*.

Almost no Mexicans appeared in Disney's *Davy Crockett: King of the Wild Frontier* until the final battle scene. As for John Wayne's *Alamo*, Texan literary critic Don Graham got it right in 1985 when he noted with a touch of irony that "the Mexican army in Wayne's film looks like a marching mass of choir boys." Graham observed that "[b]y 1960 it was no longer fashionable to resort to the simple racist contrasts" of bygone days. As if to accentuate the distance that popular culture had come since *Texas History Movies* were first drawn in the 1920s, Graham commented that the portrayal by actor J. Carroll Naish of Santa Anna in *The Last Command* (1956), the only Alamo movie produced in the interval between Parker's appearance and Wayne's, was of a vain and ambitious man, "but nonetheless a man and not a blustering cartoon."

If the classic films of the 1950s did not reflect racist conceptions of the meaning of the Alamo, what role, if any, *had* popular culture played in forming the connection that could be seen in my mail? Frankly, I was disinclined to enter the debate over the Crockett controversy's significance in American popular culture. My training and practice were in traditional documentary analysis, and I felt less than fully prepared to critique the visual images that were so important in shaping popular historical memories. Yet I began to realize that much of the attention that my own research was receiving in the media was a function not so much of its inherent worth as its public association with the historical "icon within an icon": Crockett's last stand at the Alamo.

Moreover, I felt the need to clarify my own thinking about the relationship of my historical work to the "culture wars" in which I now found myself a reluctant participant. Knowing that I had initially been fully prepared to accept Bill Groneman's accusations of forgery in *Defense of a Legend* (had his arguments been sound), I resented suggestions that anything I had written had been motivated by either crass cynicism or a desire to invent and market a "contrarian neohistory" to suit my self-interest. But I also knew that I cared deeply about the effect that my writings about the past would have on public attitudes in the present.

Tom Lindley's and Bill Groneman's own "defenses of the legend" of Davy's death against my theories (and de la Peña's allegations) seemed to me to be motivated by an honest commitment to the values of patriotism and heroism, even in the instances where I concluded that their ardor had clouded their reading of the evidence. What truly interested me were the less rational, more visceral attacks I had received—which was why I had come to Corpus Christi to look at the papers of Dan Kilgore.

I knew that Kilgore, like Carmen Perry before him and Crockett biographer Paul Andrew Hutton after him, had been accused of "dragging down a national hero" for suggesting that Crockett had been captured and executed following the Battle of the Alamo. When Carmen Perry, the translator of the de la Peña diary, heard that Kilgore was planning to publish *How Did Davy Die?*, she warned him that she had received a "suitcase" full of hostile responses "accusing *me* [she wrote] of all sorts of things I'm supposed to have said about Davy Crockett." Paul Andrew Hutton had endorsed de la Peña's story of Crockett's execution in two essays written on the occasion of the 1986 sesquicentennial of Texan independence. Hutton reported a resulting "avalanche" of outraged letters accusing him of having "a problem with heroes" (as well as with his own manhood).

Yet none of these three targets of protest had ever publicly indicated that any of the unwelcome letters in their mailboxes contained the kind of anti-Mexican sentiments I had found in my own. When I examined Kilgore's mail, some of it exhibited little in the way of racist overtones. Often, his critics were clearly defenders of the "Disney version." A lady from Minden, Louisiana, the writer who had accused Kilgore of "dragging down a national hero," told him that the "Fess Parker image has done a lot more for children than your book can." And we have already encountered the irate writer from Florida who claimed that Kilgore's book was part of a Communist plot to degrade American heroes. That letter closed with a flourish straight from Disneyland: "He's still King of the wild frontier."

Other missives from Kilgore's detractors, however, contained more elemental and disturbing themes. The writer from West Anniston, Alabama, previously mentioned, who wanted to wash Kilgore's mouth out with soap, specifically defended "white-Southern men" against any implication of cowardice. An even more pointed response to Kilgore's book came from Houston, Texas:

> The statements about Davy Crockett . . . are part of a pattern to discredit all prominent white Americans who helped to build our state and nation. Lies have been concocted and facts distorted to make all white American heroes appear to be fugitives from morals charges or rank cowards at least.
>
> Perhaps Dan Kilgore . . . will bravely lead the American charge, if any, when Omar Torrijos [a Panamanian dictator], Fidel Castro and all the Russians, Mexicans, Hindus, Chinese, Vietnamese, Iranians, Nigerians, Arabs, and South Americans make official their invasion of America and overthrow of our democratic republic.

Upon reading this letter in the Kilgore archive, I immediately recalled the accusation that my own motives in defending the de la Peña narrative were directed toward the "legitimization and glorification of the murderous scoundrels of American history, be they Indians, Mexicans, or Japanese, at the expense of our traditional, completely documented, red-blooded, heroic Anglo ancestors."

What was it about the Alamo that evoked such outbursts, with these not-so-subtle racial themes? In 1995 Paul Hutton published an insightful essay on "The Alamo as Icon" that echoed the opinion of the London *Daily Mail* that Kilgore's (and thus Hutton's own) greatest offense in questioning the mode of Crockett's demise was to tamper with a sacred national myth.*

Of course, when measured against the great battles of history, the thirteen-day siege of the Alamo, even with the total extermination of its two-hundred-odd defenders, was just what Santa Anna called it at the time: "a small affair." During the American Civil War, five thousand soldiers were killed and another eighteen thousand wounded in the span of seven hours at the Battle of Antietam. The Battle of the Somme in the First World War lasted for five months, with over a million men killed and wounded. The power of the Alamo's story, however, has never been about sheer size or numbers, but rather the dogged determination of its doomed defenders. Moreover, the mythic Alamo of the American collective imagination has become far more important than the Alamo of tedious historical fact.

The Alamo stands today as one of the cardinal icons of the American past as well as the principal symbol of the Texan identity. Why is it that (as historian Michael Kammen has noted) a nation that reveres success nevertheless elevates its great defeats,

---

*See "The Alamo as Icon" in *The Texas Military Experience*, edited by Joseph G. Dawson III and published by the Texas A&M University Press. An earlier version of Hutton's essay was published in 1985 as the introduction to *Alamo Images: Changing Perceptions of a Texas Experience*, by Susan Prendergast Schoelwer with Tom W. Gläser (DeGolyer Library and Southern Methodist University Press).

such as the Battle of the Alamo and Custer's Last Stand, to a status even more exalted than its victories? The truth is, battles in which the vanquished forces are completely obliterated have commanded exceptional respect across the pages of history. As Hutton noted in "The Alamo as Icon," many nations point proudly to such historical annihilations, whether it is the Spartan commander Leonidas holding fast at Thermopylae against the Persians or Roland slain fighting the Saracens at the mountain pass of Roncevaux—or George Armstrong Custer, overwhelmed by the Sioux at the Battle of the Little Bighorn. In all such cherished defeats, says Hutton, the heroes

> are always vastly outnumbered by a vicious enemy from a culturally inferior nation bent on the utter destruction of the heroic band's people. These men fight for their way of life in a battle that is clearly hopeless. They know that they are doomed but go willingly to their deaths in order to bleed the enemy and buy time for their people. . . . They perish with a fierce élan that turns their defeat into a spiritual victory. The leader of the defeated band is often elevated to the status of a national hero, while the battle becomes a point of cultural pride: an example of patriotism and self-sacrifice. . . . Such is clearly the case with the Alamo and its trinity of heroes: William Barret Travis, Jim Bowie, and Davy Crockett.

The death of David Crockett at the Alamo must therefore be recognized not merely as an isolated incident of trivial military significance (even if that's objectively what it was), but as a pivotal moment in what Hutton has called the "Texas creation myth," a powerful saga of "courage, sacrifice, . . . and redemption" through which shared beliefs and a common identity are expressed through succeeding generations.

Already in 1836, even before the embattled Texans had received their April deliverance with Sam Houston's stunning victory over Santa Anna at San Jacinto, they were finding in the story of the Alamo's fall their own parallel to the archetypal self-lessness of "Leonidas and his Spartan band." And they inscribed on the first Alamo monument, completed in 1841 and installed in the state capitol in 1858, this epigram: "Thermopylae had her messenger of defeat—the Alamo had none."

As an icon the Alamo has been resonant with meaning and the actions of each member of the heroic band suffused with timeless moral lessons. The mythic Alamo has become what historian Richard Slotkin calls a "deeply encoded metaphor" that immediately connects a specific historical event with a whole system of values and beliefs. The belief system conveyed by the iconic Alamo has been described by Paul Hutton in terms of associated opposites—metonymical dichotomies—through which the Texans defined themselves in stark contrast to their Mexican foes:

> As with the struggle [between Greeks and Persians] at Thermopylae, the early Texans viewed the conflict at the Alamo as a conflict of civilizations: freedom versus tyranny, democracy versus despotism, Protestantism versus Catholicism, the New World culture of the United States versus the Old World culture of Mexico, Anglo-Saxons versus the mongrelized mixture of Indian and Spanish races, and ultimately, the forces of good and evil.

Seen in this light, the manner of Crockett's death becomes a question of enormous consequence: what lessons, after all, does a hero impart who surrenders to the forces of tyranny, despotism, and evil? It was therefore with considerable surprise that I read, a bit further along in "The Alamo as Icon," Paul Hutton's explanation for the outrage expressed at the notion of Crockett's surrender—outrage that filled the letters received by Perry, Kilgore, Hutton, and myself.

Though Hutton acknowledged that the "Texas creation myth" was a product of the nineteenth century, he nevertheless argued that before the actor "Fess Parker went down swinging his rifle . . . at the advancing Mexicans" on the *Disneyland* television program in 1955, accounts of Crockett's capture and execution had been "accepted by most readers without argument." Hutton further asserted that "the story of Crockett's surrender was quite common in the nineteenth century and seemed to upset no one"—not even Theodore Roosevelt, who, said Hutton, included the "surrender story" in his *Hero Tales from American History* (1895), with no "negative reflection on Crockett." In short, Hutton saw the outrage expressed in the hate mail as essentially a post-*Disneyland* phenomenon.

As we have seen, conflicting stories of Crockett's death have coexisted since 1836, but the story of Crockett's surrender *did* upset more than a few Americans before 1955, including the prominent Texan artist Henry A. McArdle. His enormous canvas *Dawn at the Alamo*, completed in 1905, depicted Crockett in desperate hand-to-hand combat with Mexican soldiers at the most dramatic moment of the battle. McArdle branded as "ignorant or willful slanders" the suggestions that Alamo defenders had tried to surrender, or that a handful of them had "begg[ed] for their lives before Santa Anna."

Likewise, Captain Reuben M. Potter, McArdle's chief historical consultant on the details of the Alamo's fall (though Potter had not been present at the battle), was moved to protest when an 1883 article in the *Magazine of American History* implied that David Crockett had been killed after the Alamo garrison had "surrendered." Though Potter was willing to grant the possibility that a few "skulkers" had been found and killed by the Mexicans after the battle, he maintained that "[n]ot a man of that garrison surrendered, but each one, Crockett among the rest, fell fighting at his post," and that any suggestion to the contrary "does great injustice to the defenders of the Alamo."

Certainly Hutton's claim that Theodore Roosevelt's tale of heroics at the Alamo included a Crockett "surrender story" is belied by Roosevelt's own words:

> Then [wrote TR of the final scene] . . . the last man stood at bay. It was old Davy Crockett. Wounded in a dozen places, he faced his foes with his back to the wall, ringed around by the bodies of the men he had slain. So desperate was the fight he waged, that the Mexicans who thronged round him were beaten back for the moment, and no one dared to run in upon him. Accordingly, while the lancers held him where he was, for, weakened by wounds and loss of blood, he could not break through them, the musketeers loaded their carbines and shot him down. Santa Anna declined to give him mercy. Some say that when Crockett fell from his wounds, he was taken alive, and was then shot by Santa Anna's order; but his fate cannot be told with certainty, for not a single American was left alive.

There is no moment of "surrender" in this passage. Notably, the illustration of Crockett's death that accompanied Roosevelt's narrative in *Hero Tales* showed Davy still holding a pistol in his right hand—hardly a sign of surrender—as he received the fatal fire from a line of Mexican musketeers.

Hutton is by no means blind to the possibility that a racial agenda might be lurking behind a passionate defense of Crockett's heroism. As we have seen, his own description of the Alamo myth depicted a stark contest of "Anglo-Saxons" against a "mongrelized mixture of Indian and Spanish races." Still, his basic instinct is to view the letters of outrage sent to Perry and Kilgore as a defense of the "*Disneyland* Davy"—the response of a mid-twentieth-century American popular culture. Hutton might have placed a greater emphasis on the racial component

"Death of Crockett" from Hero Tales from American History *(1895), by Henry Cabot Lodge and Theodore Roosevelt.* (SOURCE: THE CENTURY COMPANY.)

of the outrage if he had read the full complement of Kilgore's protest mail. But evidently he did not, for all the letters to Kilgore he has quoted came from a newspaper column written in 1985 by Kent Biffle of the *Dallas Morning News*, an essentially light-hearted piece that featured some of Kilgore's more outspoken detractors but ignored the more distressful aspects of the correspondence.

As I read through the Kilgore letters—and my own—it seemed to me that actual contemporary voices of racial resentment and anxiety had, in effect, been "silenced" in the scholarly discussion the controversy, leaving the impression that the "hate" in the "hate mail" was directed solely toward the offending revisionist historians who dared to question Crockett's heroism. But the characterization of the Mexican as a despised and contemptible "Other" could be found not only in our hate mail, but also, if one looked closely, in the Alamo itself.

As late as the 1990s, visitors to the Alamo Shrine in San Antonio would find in the spoken and unspoken messages they received there a reinforcement of the notion lurking behind the heated rhetoric of the hate mail: that this was a battle between two fundamentally different kinds of people—"Texans" and "Mexicans." In this "binary logic" (as it has been described by anthropologist Richard R. Flores), the Tejanos were virtually erased from history. The filmstrip shown to tourists was explicitly structured along this binary vision, with brave, valiant Anglo volunteers up against the trained brigades of the ruthless Mexican dictator. But the message was also conveyed in more subtle ways. The Alamo's "Hall of Honor " displayed the flags of every country and American state that contributed defenders to the final battle. More than two dozen flags representing birthplaces in Denmark and Germany as well as every corner of the British Isles joined those of twenty-two American states, including Texas. But there was no Mexican flag so honored, obscuring the fact that nine of the eleven defenders born in Texas were Tejanos.

Even the arrangement of cacti and roses on the grounds of the Alamo has been interpreted as revealing a structured dichotomy between the natural and the cultured, the desert Southwest and the cultivated Old South—thus encapsulating (according to anthropologist Holly Beachley Brear) the central theme of the Texas creation mythology: that of Anglo order redeemed from Mexican chaos. Brear also found in the legends and ceremonies surrounding the Alamo a rigid hierarchy of race framed within a "sacred narrative" in which the Mexicans were assigned the role of "executioner" in a story of "Anglo sacrifice."*

That such messages were not lost on those who passed through the sanctified walls might best be shown by the experience of a Tejano third-grader whose class visited the Alamo on a field trip in the 1960s. As the students emerged from the ruins of the ancient chapel into the Texas sunlight, the Tejano student's best friend (an Anglo) nudged his elbow and whispered,

---

*In fairness to the present caretakers of the Alamo, it should be noted that several important changes, both substantive and symbolic, have been made at the site since Brear and Flores conducted the bulk of their fieldwork. For instance, a Mexican national flag has been added to those mounted in the "Hall of Honor," and the filmstrip that Flores found particularly objectionable was replaced in 1997 by a video with a less "binary" (and more historically accurate) presentation of the conflict.

"You killed them! You and the other mes'kins." Thus was young Richard Flores introduced to the power of the Alamo's mythic imagery. Historian Andrés Tijerina remembers a similar scene that played out in his elementary school classroom in West Texas. After his Anglo teacher had finished presenting the history of the Alamo battle, she pointed to the ten-year-old and said, "It was your grandfather, Andrés, who killed Davy Crockett!"

What were the wellsprings of this racialized mythology? When did "Remember the Alamo!" become a formula for forgetting the Tejanos' role in the Revolution and demonizing all "Mexicans"? Interestingly, the modern tradition of venerating the Alamo chapel as a shrine of patriotic sacrifice crystallized only in the last decade of the nineteenth century and the first two decades of the twentieth. As late as the 1870s, the building so cherished today was being used as a grocery warehouse to store onions and potatoes. Why, after a half-century of virtual neglect, did the Alamo (and the preservation of its ruins) become the focal point of Anglo-Texan historical consciousness between 1900 and 1915?

In part, the turn-of-the-century movement in Texas toward historic preservation and celebration as a form of "ancestor worship" reflected broader trends within the United States. Those trends placed particular emphasis on an Anglo-Saxon heritage, no doubt as a response in some measure to nationwide anxieties about newly arrived "foreign" immigrants and to unsettling changes brought about by industrialization. Yet social and economic changes specific to Texas were drastically altering the role of "Mexicans" in Texan society, and, as Texas changed socially, so did the way that Anglos depicted Mexicans.

The arrival of railroads in South Texas in the 1880s was one catalyst of socioeconomic transformation. As it became possible to ship fruits and vegetables cheaply to distant markets, new forms of commercial agriculture bloomed in former ranching counties where for generations Tejano *vaqueros* had worked cattle from horseback. With huge profits to be made from the transformed landscape, the powerful new growers' interests pushed to ensure that their seasonal laborers would be both cheap and docile. This realignment of the regional economy, especially in South Texas, assumed a distinct racial character as Mexicans were placed under a segregationist regime that was not challenged until the coming of World War II.

Institutionally, the larger transformation of society began in 1902 with the segregation of Mexicans in public schools. The imposition of a poll tax requirement for voting came in the same year and in 1904 a "White Man's Primary," also designed to suppress Mexican (and African American) political participation, was approved by the dominant Texas Democratic Party. Between 1900 and 1915 residential segregation of Tejanos increased dramatically, both in urban settings and on the vast, increasingly Anglo-dominated farms and ranches of the state.

"Symbolic forms," notes Richard Flores with regard to the Alamo as a racially charged Texan icon, "emerge from real social conditions." As the policies of segregation and disfranchisement were being carried out in Texas as well as in many Southern states undergoing their own economic transformations, observes historian David Montejano, "Texan historical memories played a part similar to Reconstruction memories in the Jim Crow South" in justifying these measures. During this time of accelerated change, images of the past often served the needs of the present. "By the early twentieth century," writes Montejano, "the story of the Alamo and Texas frontier history had become purged of its ambiguities—of the fact that Mexicans and Anglos had often fought on the same side." The complex realities of Juan Seguín's Texas Revolution, in other words, were being set aside in favor of the oversimplifications that would inform *Texas History Movies*. "Historical lessons" drawn from this mythicized Texan past were being used to define Texas race relations and to rationalize classifying Mexicans as "a colored people."

There is no better example of the use of mythic memory to demonize and marginalize both blacks and Mexicans in the early twentieth century than a pair of silent films produced by the D. W. Griffith studio in 1915: the infamous *Birth of a Nation* (which shows the Ku Klux Klan rescuing innocent whites from the evils of "Black Reconstruction") and the much lesser-known but equally racist *Birth of Texas, or Martyrs of the Alamo*. The latter film offers a simplistic racial interpretation of the Texas Revolution: a lecherous, drunken, dark-skinned Mexican soldiery so outrages the unoffending Anglo-Texans that the long-suffering colonists rise up against the evil regime that threatens to disarm their menfolk and debauch their women.

Griffith's film was hardly alone in its blatantly racist portrayal of Mexicans. As critic Don Graham has shown, there was a distinct shift around the turn of the century from an anti-Catholic to a racial theme in novels of the Texas Revolution. Mexicans, once portrayed as innocent dupes of conniving priests, were increasingly denounced as inferior, mixed-blood "Greasers," and the sentiment expressed in *Guy Raymond: A Story of the Texas*

Revolution (Houston, TX: 1908) was typical: "Mexican treachery was but one degree removed from savage barbarity." Romantic accounts of love and marriage between Anglos and Mexicans, which had been frequent in the milder and more tolerant fiction of the mid-nineteenth century, largely disappeared.

Yet this turn-of-the-century racist literature was obscure and virtually unread by the time that Dan Kilgore wrote *How Did Davy Die?* in 1978. And, though a celluloid print of the once "lost" *Martyrs of the Alamo* was discovered in 1977, the rare silent film's impact on Kilgore's public was utterly insignificant. The angry folks who were sending hate mail to those of us who dared to argue that Crockett had been executed were not getting their racially charged inspiration from these obscure sources. Other than the sometimes subtle biases that Brear and Flores found encoded in the messages surrounding the Alamo shrine itself, does there remain in Texan popular culture today any tangible legacy of the early twentieth century's militantly racist mythology?

Ironically, one need not look further than the dust jacket of *How Did Davy Die?* for a clue to an important source of this troubling legacy. For, despite Kilgore's conclusion that Davy died by execution, there on the cover is Crockett locked in mortal combat with brutish Mexicans. The scene was lifted from Henry A. McArdle's 1905 painting *Dawn at the Alamo*. This is the same image of Crockett that Andrés Tijerina singled out for attention in his interview with the BBC at the state capitol. (The entire painting is reproduced as Color Plate One in this book.)

To double the irony, when Paul Hutton first endorsed the de la Peña account of Crockett's execution, his essay appeared

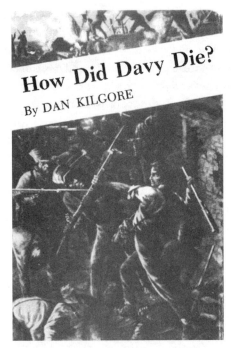

Cover of How Did Davy Die? *(1978), by Dan Kilgore.* (COPYRIGHT: TEXAS A&M UNIVERSITY PRESS.)

in a book whose cover, once again, featured Davy going down swinging, this time as portrayed in Robert Jenkins Onderdonk's 1903 masterpiece, *The Fall of the Alamo*. (Shown here as Color Plate Two.)*

---

*The irony continues. My thoughts about the decision to put Onderdonk's powerful but problematic painting on the cover of *Sleuthing the Alamo* are set forth, in essence, in the last three pages of the present chapter (pp. 176–178).

Today these two "canonical" paintings by the rival San Antonio artists hang in places of exceptional honor: Onderdonk's *The Fall of the Alamo* in the Governor's Mansion in Austin and McArdle's *Dawn at the Alamo* in the Senate Chamber of the Texas State Capitol. Reproductions of both, furthermore, are found everywhere in Texas. When artist Eric von Schmidt began research in the early 1980s for his own rendition of the Alamo defenders' last stand, he found that Onderdonk's version of Crockett's death had achieved a "quasi-official" status and a predominant place in contemporary articles and textbooks. McArdle's canvas is almost as familiar to Texans. Buyers of Sam DeShong Ratcliffe's comprehensive survey, *Painting Texas History to 1900* (published in 1992), found a two-hundred-square-inch, full-color reproduction of McArdle's giant canvas wrapped around their purchase as its dust jacket.

As different as these two paintings may appear, their common *iconography*—their specific visual references to the doomed defense of the Alamo—is obvious. Although Onderdonk's striking composition focuses the viewer's attention in a way that the crowded canvas of McArdle cannot, each painter has chosen the moment of Crockett's last stand for his depiction of the Alamo's fall.

What may not be so obvious is that the two paintings also share a common *iconology*—that is, a similarity in the graphic expression of the artists' values and attitudes and, arguably, the attitudes of the audience for whom they were creating their works. When contrasted to earlier representations of the fall of the Alamo in Texan art, these two paintings reveal not only a heightened emphasis on the garrison's refusal to surrender, but also a much harsher depiction of the Mexican as a despicable creature standing in stark contrast to the doomed but majestic Alamo defenders. Each in its own style portrays a struggle between the forces of light and darkness, of good and evil.

It is remarkable that Texans came almost as tardily to an artistic portrayal of the Alamo's fall as they did to the preservation of the last remains of the old mission. One of the first to tackle the subject was Theodore Gentilz, a French immigrant to the Republic of Texas who settled in San Antonio in the mid-1840s. He painted a bird's-eye view of the battle around 1885, carefully recreating the architecture of the Alamo but with a perspective so remote as to render both attackers and defenders little more than stick figures.

However, in the 1890s Gentilz offered a closer look at the Mexicans who captured the Alamo in his *Death of Dickinson*, which shows a well-disciplined, neatly uniformed, and relatively light-complexioned soldiery awaiting orders from General Santa Anna before executing a Texan defender who is attempting to surrender. The artist has portrayed the Mexicans in the style of a Napoleonic army. (See Color Plate Three.)

Lest Gentilz be accused of atypical politeness in his portrayal of Mexicans due to his European origin, his images should be compared to those of two early Anglo-Texan artists. Despite its grim title, Louis Eyth's *Death of Bowie: A Command from the Mexicans that He Be Killed* (dating from the 1870s) shows a restrained group of handsome Mexican soldiers commanded by an officer of noble bearing. (See p. 159.)

Although artist Charles McLaughlin did not paint a scene from the Alamo, he had himself joined a Texan expedition

Death of Bowie: A Command from the Mexicans that He Be Killed
(ca. 1878), by Louis Eyth. (Location of original drawing unknown.)

against Mexico in 1842 and was captured and held prisoner for
months in the interior of Mexico. An eyewitness to most of the
events he delineated, McLaughlin portrayed the Mexican soldiers
in scene after scene very much in the same fashion as Theodore
Gentilz and Louis Eyth. Were it not for the Mexicans' uniforms
(and their fondness for thin *mostachos*), it would be very difficult to tell the two sides apart. (See p. 160.)

The same could never be said for the Mexicans of Onderdonk
and McArdle, though their compositional techniques are quite
distinct. Onderdonk is the more subtle of the two, using shadow
and light, clothing as well as skin tone, and crouching Mexicans
versus a fully erect Crockett to achieve a striking contrast between

Texian Charge Upon the Guards & Victory at Salado *(1845), by Charles McLaughlin. From* Journal of the Texian Expedition Against Mier, *by Gen. Thomas J. Green.* (COPYRIGHT: LIBRARY OF TEXAS, DeGOLYER LIBRARY, SOUTHERN METHODIST UNIVERSITY.)

the contending forces. But this painting also carries a thoroughly unsubtle visual allusion. Texan viewers in 1903, as well as the visitors to the St. Louis World's Fair who saw Onderdonk's painting on display at the Texas Pavilion in 1904, would recognize in the portrayal of Crockett an unmistakable reference to another last stand: that of George Armstrong Custer at the Battle of the Little Bighorn in 1876.

The figure of Crockett in Onderdonk's painting is a virtual mirror image of General Custer in Otto Becker's *Custer's Last Fight*, a lithograph distributed nationwide in 1896 by the Anheuser-Busch Brewing Company. By the turn of the century, this example of "saloon art" was one of the most famous images in America. (The lithograph is shown in Color Plate Four.)

Becker's image, even more than the original painting on which it was based, was designed to emphasize the utter annihilation of the forces of civilization by a savage foe. All about Custer's troops, Sioux Indian warriors surge forward. For Cassilly Adams, who created the original painting, that prospect was fearsome aplenty. But when Otto Becker created a lithograph based on Adams's work, apparently the Indian attackers were not quite enough. Becker added three or four new warriors, with headgear and shields that were utterly foreign to the Sioux—utterly foreign because Becker had inserted African Zulu warriors! During the Anglo-Zulu War of 1879, three years after Custer's defeat by the Sioux in the American West, a British force in southern Africa had been wiped out to the last man by the Zulu at the Battle of Isandhlwana. The two shield-bearing Zulu who may be clearly seen in the lithograph rushing toward Custer's back appear to have been lifted by Becker from engravings of scenes from the Anglo-Zulu War that were published in *The Illustrated London News.* (See p. 162.)

Why would Onderdonk model his Crockett figure on Becker's Custer? It may have been due to the wishes of his patron, a Texas businessman and amateur historian named James Thomas DeShields, who commissioned Onderdonk to create an Alamo painting in 1901. A small initial sketch for the "Death of Crockett" that Onderdonk sent to DeShields for his approval in that year is clearly the prototype for *The Fall of the Alamo,* but the Crockett figure in it shows far less congruence with Becker's hero than does the final version. (See p. 163.)

DeShields treasured the finished product—he owned the completed canvas until his death in 1948—and, significantly, al-

Detail of Zulu warriors from Otto Becker's lithograph (after Cassilly Adams) of Custer's Last Fight *(1896).* (COPYRIGHT: AMON CARTER MUSEUM, FT. WORTH, TEXAS.)

ways referred to it as *Crockett's Last Fight,* apparently wanting both the name of his painting and the figure in its title role to invoke the spirit of the hero of the Little Bighorn. In 1986 artist Eric von Schmidt described the tight similarity between the heroes in *Crockett's Last Fight* and *Custer's Last Fight* for the *Smithsonian* magazine (compare Color Plates Two and Four):

> If you reverse the mythically potent Custer over the figure of Crockett in Onderdonk's *Alamo,* you have a near-perfect fit. Both are complete with legendary yellow-tinted buckskins, legendary red bandannas, and even their legendary trademarks at full brandish: George's saber, Davy's long rifle.

Robert Jenkins Onderdonk, sketch for "Crockett's Last Stand," 1901 (preliminary sketch for The Fall of the Alamo, *1903).* (COPYRIGHT: DALLAS MUSEUM OF ART, GIFT OF ELEANOR ONDERDONK.)

No excess of imagination was required to complete the equation: the "swarthy foes" showing "demoniac expressions mingled with fear" (as the Mexicans were described by admiring contemporary critics of Onderdonk's work) were about to sweep over Crockett, even as the Sioux had overcome the noble Custer and as the Zulu had engulfed the British fighters at Isandhlwana. These linked depictions of dark and savage enemies also help to explain why the notion of Crockett's surrender to the Mexicans at the Alamo is so vehemently rejected by those who would lump together all such "murderous scoundrels." Both Crockett and Custer bore what the British imperial poet Rudyard Kipling referred to as "the White Man's Burden." For self and for civilization, this had to be a fight to the finish. Surrender (from this perspective) was unthinkable, and captivity, worse than death.

There is a curious inversion going on here, as historian Richard White has pointed out. The nineteenth century witnessed the culmination of four hundred years of expansion and conquest by Europeans of the North American continent and its native peoples. As the last remnants of the frontier were disappearing, audiences in the United States and Europe thrilled to the performances mounted by the former scout Buffalo Bill Cody and his "Wild West Show." His dramas, suggested White, "presented an account of Indian aggression and white defense; of Indian killers and white victims; of, in effect, badly abused conquerors." In order to achieve a guiltless conquest, argued White, "Americans had to transform conquerors into victims. The great military icons of American westward expansion are not victories, they are defeats: the Alamo and the Battle of the Little Bighorn. We, these stories say, do not plan our conquests. . . . We just retaliate against barbaric massacres."

In the 1870s San Antonio artist Henry A. McArdle set aside his own monumental Alamo project in order to complete instead an equally giant painting of the Battle of San Jacinto (which now shares the west wall of the Texas Senate Chamber with his *Dawn at the Alamo*). McArdle wanted to make full use, before it was too late, of the eyewitness recollections of the many surviving Texan veterans of the Revolution's final battle. In 1895 he completed *The Battle of San Jacinto*, a work in which McArdle strove for precise realism in the depiction of both the battle site and the participants.

When Robert J. Onderdonk's newly finished painting of Crockett at the Alamo went on display in San Antonio in 1903, it created something of a sensation. Not wanting to be outdone by his crosstown rival, McArdle returned in that year to his own long-delayed Alamo project, for which he had done a preliminary sketch as early as 1874. (See p. 167 for sketch.)

When the new version of *Dawn at the Alamo* emerged from McArdle's studio in 1905, Onderdonk's thirty-five-square-foot canvas had been surpassed not only in size, but also in the graphic delineation of Mexican depravity. (See Color Plate One.) Art historians have commented on the lurid quality of McArdle's Mexicans, calling them "apelike" and "plasticene, psychotic murderers." One of these brutes is grappling with Davy Crockett, whose whiteness and noble bearing are highlighted by the artist's technique. For critic Emily F. Cutrer, this crude Mexican and Crockett were not merely two men, but had become "two races that represent opposing forces in the painter's mind."

At the dramatic heart of the picture, a leering Mexican soldier is about to thrust a bayonet into the back of an unsuspecting William Barret Travis, the commander of the beleaguered Alamo garrison. (See p. 166 for Crockett and Travis.)

It is perhaps indicative of the deteriorating position of Mexicans in early twentieth-century Texas that this leering caricature of a Mexican infantryman does not appear at all in McArdle's original sketch of the scene. Instead, as Captain

Detail of Crockett fight from Dawn at the Alamo *(1905), by Henry Arthur McArdle.* (COPYRIGHT: STATE PRESERVATION BOARD, AUSTIN, TEXAS.)

Detail of Travis scene from Dawn at the Alamo *(1905), by Henry Arthur McArdle.* (COPYRIGHT: STATE PRESERVATION BOARD, AUSTIN, TEXAS.)

Reuben M. Potter observed in his 1874 analysis of this earlier, more evenhanded version, "Travis is seen in a death grapple with a Mexican standard bearer, a struggle in which both are going down along with the banner which its bearer had vainly attempted to plant." (See detail on p. 168.)

There are no obvious visual clues in the original sketch of this death struggle to tell the viewer which of the combatants is the Mexican; likewise, the soldiers contending with Crockett in this early version of *Dawn at the Alamo* are neither bestialized nor are they dramatically darkened, as are the brutes who are on display today in the Senate Chamber of the Texas State Capitol.

Preliminary sketch for Dawn at the Alamo *(1874), by Henry Arthur McArdle. (Original destroyed.)* (Photograph copyright: Texas State Library and Archives Commission.)

Detail of Travis and Crockett scenes from preliminary sketch for Dawn at the Alamo *(1874), by Henry Arthur McArdle. (Original destroyed.)* (PHOTOGRAPH COPYRIGHT: TEXAS STATE LIBRARY AND ARCHIVES COMMISSION.)

In retrospect, the changes between 1874 and 1905 in both Texan social contours and Texan art seem obvious to us. But was this emerging negativity in the portrayal of Mexicans something that Texans (or Tejanos) were aware of at the time? A possible answer is suggested by evidence of a "crime" that came to light only in the spring of 1999, as I was trying to learn more about Robert Onderdonk's patron, the somewhat mysterious amateur historian James T. DeShields. I was struck by the fact that DeShields turned out to have been a patron of Louis Eyth and Henry A. McArdle, as well. As one of my newfound colleagues in the world of Texan art history put it, "all the strings seem to lead back to DeShields."

James T. DeShields (1861–1948). (Photograph copyright: DeGolyer Library, Southern Methodist University.)

I had been aware of DeShields from his numerous amateur works on the history of early Anglo-Texans, written between the 1880s and the 1930s, all in a distinctly heroic mode. As I discovered his interest in art and read the few letters of his at the DRT Library at the Alamo, I was surprised at just how little material had apparently survived from the literary and artistic life of this very influential man.

My efforts to find caches of his personal papers in other libraries or museums were futile. I could dredge up only a single scholarly article written about DeShields in 1990—and it yielded no further clues to missing materials. Yet I was loathe to give up the hunt. I suppose that I was bothered, like Sherlock Holmes, by a "dog that didn't bark": it seemed there should be more to this story than what I was finding. So in March 1999 I set aside several days to snoop around Dallas, the city where DeShields spent the last half of his life. I wasn't sure what I was searching for, but I made a list of the places that I would look, including the Dallas Museum of Art, the Dallas Historical Society, the files of the *Dallas Morning News*, and the collections of the DeGolyer Library at Southern Methodist University. To my great good fortune, I went to this last place first.

When I asked the staff archivist and her assistant if there could possibly be any material on the early Texas artists and their chief patron, James T. DeShields, both pairs of eyebrows immediately shot up. The chills in my spine were not far behind.

It turned out that not long before, DeShields' daughter (an alumna of Southern Methodist), had moved to a retirement home in San Antonio. When she left Dallas, she gave the De-Golyer Library six boxes of her father's papers that had been shoved under a bed when he died in 1948. Six boxes! The library was still in the early stages of processing the varied materials in the collection—books, pamphlets, photographs, manuscripts, personal papers—and had not yet made public their recent acquisition. I was beginning to salivate.

For the next three days, I plowed through those six boxes. On the morning of the third day, I found gold. Box number four contained the complete manuscript of a book that DeShields was working on when he died—a biography of David Crockett! In 1948 the author was in the midst of negotiations with publishers and was selecting illustrations for the book that never saw the light of day. One of the illustrations, of course, was to be the painting that hung on DeShields' own living-room wall: Onderdonk's *The Fall of the Alamo*. In the midst of the unpublished biography was a single loose, unnumbered page on which DeShields, as he neared the end of his long life, had typed out an enigmatic caption for the famed image of his hero's final moments:

CROCKETT'S LAST FIGHT

And they say hero worship comes from the love of freedom!

Years ago, the celebrated artist, R. J. Onderdonk, was commissioned to paint a scene depicting "Davy Crockett's Fight at the Alamo." That picture is an inspiration, and is one of the great historical battle pieces of America. It should have a permanent place in the Alamo.

(As a matter of fact, the archives of the Alamo Library contain two letters written by DeShields in 1947 offering without success to sell the canvas to that institution.)

De Shields concluded his caption for the Onderdonk painting with this tantalizing paragraph:

And here a bit of interesting history touching upon the vicissitude of this famous picture. Once, it was exhibited in a certain Texas city where many Mexicans lived. It was noted that such visitors to the gallery, expressed anger, sometimes with clenched fists and vehement gestures, at certain figures in the picture. When the painting was cased, awaiting transportation, and at an unguarded moment, some miscreant Mexican with knife, slit places in the canvas.

Today this is still all we know about the "crime" from DeShields, Onderdonk, or any other contemporary source. We don't even know for sure when or where it is alleged to have happened, though the best guess is March 1903, when the newly completed painting was put on display at the Adameck art store in downtown San Antonio. The records of the Bexar County jail show no one incarcerated for the slashing, which was in any event probably discovered only when the shipping case was opened. The English-language newspapers of San Antonio are silent as to the incident, and not one copy of the single Spanish-language newspaper published in San Antonio in 1903 has survived from that year.

Should this story be believed? It sounds at first almost too good to be true, especially since DeShields was trying to sell his painting to the Alamo. Was he hoping to give the artwork an aura of intrigue and tempestuous violence? Imagine the headline: "Art Imitates Life: Miscreant Mexicans Attack Davy Once Again!" Could DeShields be romanticizing the past in the style of his popular Texas histories, such as *Tall Men with Long Rifles* (1935), while at the same time attempting to make a virtue of his painting's compromised physical condition?

Without question, the painting had suffered substantial damage. This became clear when I obtained the initial examination report and the subsequent treatment report prepared for the Kimball Art Museum and the Friends of the Governor's Mansion during the restoration process in 1981. The painting had been donated by an (officially) anonymous family on the condition that it always hang in the mansion's Grand Foyer, where it remains today.

The reports describe three large tears (which had been repeatedly but clumsily repaired over the previous eight decades) on the lower right-hand quarter of the painting, totaling several feet of sliced canvas. Perhaps significantly, all of the damage is in the general area of the painting that depicts the Mexican army. But the photographs of the damage that accompany the reports reveal a strange and unexpected pattern: the "slashes" were all perfectly parallel and horizontal! (The middle slit, which both begins and ends slightly farther to the right side of the painting than the other two, has a short interruption toward its right-hand extremity.)

Could this be evidence of an act of ardent protest? In the words of Sara P. McElroy, Conservator at the Blanton Museum of Art at the University of Texas at Austin, the odd configura-

Outline drawing: location of slashes to The Fall of the Alamo. (Courtesy James E. Crisp.)

tion of the slits would suggest an unbelievably meticulous and eccentric slasher. At first glance accidental damage appears to be a far more likely explanation, perhaps from an unfortunate mishap while the painting was being moved. But a closer inspection of the damaged canvas—made possible by the data collected by Sara McElroy herself when she was a conservation intern at Fort Worth's Kimball Art Museum in 1981 (and shared with me in her Austin laboratory on a sunny day in May of 1999)—tells a different story.

Sara worked on this painting for months at the Kimball, and the slides, prints, microscopic photographs, and analytical reports that she prepared constitute today our best evidence for evaluating the reliability of DeShields' account. According to McElroy's analysis, the cleanly slit fibers revealed during the 1981 restoration indicate that the blade that did the damage was very thin and very sharp. It punctured the canvas completely at the beginning of the first rip, only to be withdrawn at the end of the sideward thrust and then plunged in for a second and a third time—with each tear perfectly horizontal and all three parallel to one another.

Here we must recall the only other evidence of the slashing—the words of DeShields' caption: "When the painting was cased, awaiting transportation, and at an unguarded moment, some miscreant Mexican with knife, slit places in the canvas." How could one possibly slit a canvas that had been cased? The answer comes only after understanding that a century ago, it was common practice to cover a painting with wooden slats in order to ship it. Plywood was introduced only in 1905, and was not man-

PLATE ONE Dawn at the Alamo, *by Henry Arthur McArdle (1905).* (COURTESY OF THE STATE PRESERVATION BOARD, AUSTIN, TEXAS. CHA 1989.81, PHOTOGRAPHER JACK MINOR, 9/92, PRE CONSERVATION.)

PLATE TWO   The Fall of the Alamo, *by Robert Jenkins Onderdonk* (1903).   (COURTESY OF THE FRIENDS OF THE GOVERNOR'S MANSION, AUSTIN, TEXAS.)

PLATE THREE *Death of Dickinson, by Theodore Gentilz (1896).* (COURTESY OF DAUGHTERS OF THE RE-
PUBLIC OF TEXAS LIBRARY AT THE ALAMO, SAN ANTONIO.)

PLATE FOUR Custer's Last Fight, *after Cassilly Adams (chromolithograph by Otto Becker, 1896).* (COURTESY OF THE AMON CARTER MUSEUM, FT. WORTH, TEXAS.)

ufactured extensively until the First World War. If the casing were not solid, a thin, sharp blade could indeed be inserted between the slats to make horizontal, parallel tears.

Thus the material evidence appears to corroborate the testimony of DeShields. And there seems also no reason to doubt his (somewhat superficial) description of the incident's *social* circumstances: Mexican "visitors to the gallery, expressed anger, sometimes with clenched fists and vehement gestures, at certain figures in the picture." Why? The Tejanos who shook their fists at *The Fall of the Alamo* in 1903 had good reason to be upset. They were witnessing—in the symbolic depiction of the Mexican army as a savage horde—a significant step in the tendentious reconstruction of the Texan past. Before their eyes, a new historical mythology was being produced. History was not being rewritten. It was being repainted.

For that reason this obscure incident in San Antonio should be of interest not only to art sleuths and antiquarians, but also to anyone concerned about how public depictions of the past mold popular attitudes of the present. The revelation of the unknown slasher's desperate action should redirect our attention to the malignant message that he (or she) seems to have seen in this painting—a painting that has probably had a greater impact on the collective Texan memory (and thus on the Texan identity) than any textbook or academic history published in the twentieth century. The racialized rewriting of Texas history carried out around the turn of the last century would cast long shadows across the next hundred years. Indeed, some of them still fall upon us today.

This is especially so because these two works of Onderdonk and McArdle are displayed today in the most privileged positions of legislative and executive power in Texas. Their presence raises perplexing questions. Do they lend inspiration to today's Texans (and Americans) by recalling the sacrifices of 1836? Or do they tragically divide these same groups by tacitly affirming the stark racial divisions of the early 1900s? What do these very public images of the past "teach" those who view them? Could they, with critical interpretation, teach a great deal more? Or should images that are considered patently offensive by large groups of the public simply be removed?

These were the questions on our lips as almost twenty of us— historians, anthropologists, art critics, conservators, museum curators, novelists, film makers, and media representatives— stepped into the Governor's Mansion on May 28, 1999, to watch as Onderdonk's painting was put under ultraviolet light in order to reveal the areas that had been restored in 1981. We had just come from a long and contentious luncheon held to discuss the newly discovered slashing and what its implications might be.

The group that I had pulled together for this informal seminar and field trip included Professor Andrés Tijerina, whose comment to the BBC interviewer two years earlier had triggered my re-examination of these all-too-familiar paintings. His chief complaint against Onderdonk's classic work was that its imagery of stalwart Anglo defenders attacked by swarthy Mexican soldiers completely erased the Tejano presence in the Texas Revolution from the public's historical consciousness.

Davy Crockett, he reminded us, had been in Texas for only four months when he died. Who then, were the real "Texans" in 1836?

Should the painting come down? My personal inclination, given such problematic images, would be to rely on addition rather than subtraction. Historians bear a special responsibility to bring to the public voices from the past that have remained silenced or ignored by the mainstream culture. Rather than remove *The Fall of the Alamo* from the Governor's Mansion, I would prefer to seize the opportunity provided by the long-silenced slasher to inform visitors about the circumstances of 1903 as well as those of 1836—and thus to ask them to think more deeply about their state's past and its present than embarrassed silence, heavy-handed censorship, or uncritical celebration would ever demand of them.

Such a presentation would also force them to think about "history" (as opposed to "the past") as something that is *made*, not *found*. The circumstances under which history is produced, moreover, inevitably leave their mark. This is why it is worthwhile today to view a film like D. W. Griffith's *Martyrs of the Alamo*, which as movie historian Frank Thompson observes, tells us much more about 1915 than it does about 1836. It is for precisely these reasons that I presented from my childhood some of the painful and long-censored images from *Texas History Movies* displayed in the prologue of this book.

In the final paragraph of her book *Inherit the Alamo: Myth and Ritual at an American Shrine*, Holly Brear offers this advice from a "responsible anthropologist":

> The first step in resolving conflict between ethnicities comes in re-thinking the created divisions between groups, especially in historical narratives. . . . Examining the roles we assign one another in our sacred narratives allows us to view the hierarchical construction of these roles and to question their "naturalness."

We should never allow even the most revered of our society's "sacred narratives" to be accepted as simple truths, nor to be mistaken for legitimate history. Myths offer the false comfort of simplicity, and this simplicity is accomplished by the selective silencing of the past. Ironically, when it comes to this kind of silencing, the paintbrush can become a more lethal weapon than the knife.

Afterword

The Silence of the Yellow Rose

WHENEVER HISTORICAL NARRATORS TAKE UP THE PEN (OR the paintbrush) in order to bring the past to the present, one thing is sure: someone else has beaten them to the punch. Historical narration begins long before the historian or the artist arrives on the scene. It begins simultaneously with the historical action itself, because actors *in* history are also narrators *of* history.

As a case in point, take the participants in the Texas Revolution. We know that General Santa Anna "won" the Battle of the Alamo on March 6, 1836, only to lose disastrously to Sam Houston's rebels at San Jacinto less than seven weeks later. But Santa Anna lost *two* battles on April 21. According to anthropologist Michel-Rolph Trouillot, Santa Anna

was doubly defeated at San Jacinto. He lost the battle of the day, but he also lost the battle he had won at the Alamo. Houston's men had punctuated their victorious attack on the Mexican army with repeated shouts of "Remember the Alamo! Remember the Alamo!" With that reference to the old mission, they doubly made history. As actors, they captured Santa Anna and neutralized his forces. As narrators, they gave the Alamo story a new meaning. The military loss of March was no longer the end point of the narrative but a necessary turn in the plot, the trial of heroes, which, in turn, made final victory both inevitable and grandiose.

In the storyline of the Texas Revolution created by San Jacinto's winners, the battle of the Alamo takes on a very different significance than in the tale told by the war's losers—even if the one telling that tale is José Enrique de la Peña, whose outrage at the carnage at San Antonio, as we have seen, was quite unlike the reaction of his commander.

Santa Anna's defeat at San Jacinto meant that he would not have the power to "dictate" the accepted history of what had happened at the Alamo. While it is a truism to say that "the winners write the history," Trouillot goes beyond this cliché in his book *Silencing the Past: Power and the Production of History* (1995), to insist that while "any narrative history is a particular bundle of silences," still "not all silences are equal."

In other words, though every narrator must make choices in selecting which facts are to be included and the significance attributed to them, sometimes what is *not* said—*not* included in the narrative—is actually the most important part of the story as experienced by many of those who lived it. Not everyone's story gets told, and even when told, not everyone's story is heard. The production and distribution of historical narratives is bound up with relationships of power—relationships that make some narratives possible (or even dominant), but that silence others.

De la Peña would have no trouble understanding the implication of Trouillot's title, *Silencing the Past: Power and the Production of History*. The Mexican junior officer went up against men of great power, and they silenced him. Prison, poverty, illness, and an early death meant the defeat of his effort to affect the course of Mexican history by becoming an historian. He wanted to publish his narrative in order to assure that the blame for the loss of Texas would fall only upon those politicians and generals who deserved it. Though de la Peña failed in his attempt, it was not because his narrative wasn't powerful. It's because *he* wasn't powerful.

Note that de la Peña's intention to "make history" with the pen instead of the sword reveals that the equation works in both directions: just as actors *in* history are also narrators *of* history, so too do narrators become actors. In other words, the producers of "history"—of historical narratives—can affect "history" in the sense of the actual course of events. They do this by influencing the thoughts, and therefore the actions, of their audience. The two kinds of "history"—what has happened and what is said to have happened—are distinct but intertwined.

The production of this second kind of history is a complex process that hides behind the apparently simple presentation of the historical "facts." It may be useful to remember that the word *fact* is a linguistic relative to the (very) active verbs of *to do* and *to make*. (Another related word is *manufacture*.) In the *making* of facts, Trouillot describes four analytically separate "moments:" *creation, assembly, retrieval,* and *delivery*. At each of these steps in the production of history, the silencing of disfavored or unlucky voices can (and usually does) occur. De la Peña's own voice is a perfect example: it was subjected to some manner of silencing at each step along the way.

The first of Trouillot's "moments" is the moment of fact *creation*, or "the making of sources." In countless instances, potential sources of our historical knowledge have been eliminated by death, poverty, disease, enslavement, execution, illiteracy, prison, or any other of the dire circumstances that can destroy a story before it ever exists—simply by destroying its creator's ability to relate it. General Manuel Castrillón, lying dead on the San Jacinto battlefield, could not tell the victors what had happened to Davy Crockett, much less what Castrillón thought of Santa Anna's interrupted march across Texas. Herman Ehrenberg lost his diary when he plunged into the San Antonio River to flee what he called the "murder of the prisoners" at Goliad; but because the Mexican bullets missed the young soldier, he lived to write his memoir (and to castigate his assailants).

De la Peña's diary as well as his memoir survived his imprisonment and death, but they remained silenced in the next "moment"—that of fact *assembly*, or the "making of archives." As the Mexican generals and politicians published their book-length *diarios* and *historias*, de la Peña's manuscripts disappeared from sight for almost 120 years. If he had "donated" them to a government archive, they might well have disappeared forever. He did manage to publish, from prison, *Una Víctima del Despotismo*, but as we have seen, only one copy is known to have survived, and it lay dormant for yet another forty years in a quiet corner of Yale's Sterling Memorial Library, its relevance to the Texas Revolution and de la Peña's larger work unrecognized.

Archives, it should be pointed out, are for the most part created by powerful people and interests. Governments and wealthy individuals who accumulate vast collections of documents for the use of researchers have usually been motivated by patriotism, piety, or an allegiance to a particular narrative of the past. The historical legacies of the powerless, the dissenting, and the despised infrequently make it through the heavy archive doors, and seldom under their own name. Their stories, when they exist in these repositories, must often be found by indirection, amid the commentaries of the more successful, the more legitimate, the more "important." Their fragmentary remains are what the political scientist James C. Scott calls the "hidden transcripts"— sometimes not even actual voices, but only the reflections of voices. We have seen such reflections in James T. DeShields' caption for *The Fall of the Alamo*, which mentions the clenched fists of the Tejanos who protested Onderdonk's painting, and in the truly silent but more violent protest of the alleged "miscreant Mexican with knife."

The third moment is that of fact *retrieval*, or the "making of narratives." This is when the historians make their appearance. But even after the Mexican antiques dealer Jesús Sánchez Garza had rescued de la Peña's manuscript "from the dust of forgetfulness" and hundreds of copies of Sánchez Garza's *La Rebelión de Texas* were sitting on library shelves in Mexico and the United States, few paid any attention. When documents and the stories that they tell do not fit neatly into conventional categories of thought or dominant attitudes toward the past, they tend to be ignored or trivialized. Remember Lon Tinkle's reaction to de la Peña in *Thirteen Days to Glory*, his famous Alamo book of 1958. Without even having looked at *La Rebelión de Texas* carefully enough to get the name or title correct in his bibliography, he completely dismissed its contents while giving lip service to its importance.

The fact that de la Peña's testament was composed in Spanish meant that it remained silent in the United States far longer than otherwise would have been the case, and we have seen that various mistranslations, in the cases of both de la Peña and Ehrenberg, distorted their narratives and confused those historians who relied on them. When "complete" published translations finally became available, even careful and diligent editors like Carmen Perry and Henry Nash Smith made questionable decisions about the deletion of materials that, had they been published in English, would have saved scholars from innumerable errors.

Ehrenberg was silenced *twice* when Charlotte Churchill's translation was published in Dallas in 1935. Henry Smith, the editor of the text, apparently eliminated passages that he considered to be repetitive, tedious, or unreliable. In each case, ellipses mark the spot for the careful reader where these portions were deleted. But then the publisher William Tardy went through the memoir again, surreptitiously removing any items that might be considered offensive. In doing so, he not only silenced Ehrenberg, but also deceived countless readers (including many historians) who assumed the integrity of the text.

The silencing of duly archived materials in the production of new narratives frequently occurs as a result of incomplete research and/or incautious scholarship. Texan author Gary Brown recently published two books, on the New Orleans Grays and James W. Fannin, which inevitably led him to the memoir of Herman Ehrenberg. The young German described being surprised by General Urrea's onrushing cavalry as he and a few companions were serving as Fannin's rear guard during the retreat from Goliad. Because Brown could find no evidence that Ehrenberg ever returned to Texas following his departure after the Revolution, he concluded that the young soldier felt such shame for his part in the capture of Fannin's forces that he could never again face his companions in arms.

But Brown's characterization of Ehrenberg's memoir as the work of a discredited exile—a man ashamed to show his face in Texas—is flawed at its core. Ehrenberg *did* return to Texas and he did *not* avoid the company of his fellow veterans. Brown didn't thoroughly check the passenger lists of ships passing between New Orleans and Texas, and he failed to track down the land claims for military service that Ehrenberg made in Houston (in person, with fellow veterans on hand to vouch for his identity) in 1838. Brown also did not realize (because the military records in the Texas State Archives were at the time inadequately indexed) that Ehrenberg had served as a citizen-soldier in the "Pitkin Guards," a militia company organized in Houston in 1840 for service on the Texas frontier.

It was an illness contracted during this frontier service that sent Ehrenberg back to Europe for his health, where in 1842 he wrote what is clearly the testament of a proud citizen of the Texas Republic. This is in fact how he identifies himself on the book's title page: *Bürger der Republik*. What is most valuable about his narrative of the Revolution is that it opens a window onto the emerging historical and national consciousness of the Texans— seen through the eyes of a teenaged private who, as a young man with emerging political passions, tried to explain to his European readers why he had decided to adopt (and fight for) a new, democratic homeland to which he planned to return. Ehrenberg's unquestioning acceptance of slavery in the new Texas, as well as the racist anti-Mexican language that he inserted into the mouth of Sam Houston in his memoir, however, also give us a glimpse of a "darker" side of the Texas Republic.

The twisted fate of Ehrenberg's narrative shows us that even a white Teutonic Protestant male who fought on the winning side and survived to prosper could fall victim to the "silencing of the past." But more often than not, those in the ranks of the silenced are from other, less privileged categories. Even their presence in the archives by no means guarantees their inclusion in the narratives of most "Western" nations.

Trouillot, who is himself Haitian-born, notes that despite the fact that Haiti was France's wealthiest colony under the name *Saint-Domingue*—and despite the fact that Napoleon lost nineteen French generals there, including his brother-in-law—the Haitian Revolution is hardly mentioned in French histories. The loss of Haiti triggered the sale of Louisiana; more French troops died there than at Waterloo. But a successful *black* revolution that revealed the limits of the French Revolution's promise of "liberty, fraternity, and equality" (as well as the limits of French power) has been treated by French historians with a level of neglect that amounts to "the near total erasure of Haiti, slavery, and colonization" from their country's history. Silencing the inconvenient and disturbing past is the monopoly of no nation. Neither is racism.

We have already seen in this book the virtual elimination of Juan Seguín and his fellow Tejanos from the histories—and the historical paintings—produced in Texas until the very recent past. And black Texans—whether slave or free—tended until the late twentieth century to be present only in condescension or caricature. In his book *The Landscape of History: How Historians Map the Past* (2002), John Lewis Gaddis notes that the past is sometimes "uprooted" by narrators who would seek "to marginalize or even eliminate something [they don't] like in the present by rewriting history." Such erasures, observes Gaddis, often accompany efforts to "imagine a community" in such a way that those who are not a part of the chosen people are excluded or persecuted.

What is the historian's obligation to people who have been "erased," whether by malice, thoughtlessness, or ignorance? Holly Brear, the author of *Inherit the Alamo*, insists (as we saw at the end of the last chapter) that anthropologists have an obligation to their own cultures to examine what "history" means to those projecting it and how such history is used. And while she does not believe that it is for anthropologists "to determine what happened" in the past, she might be comforted to know that the surviving archival record of the Texas Revolution defies the stark ethnic divisions of the "Alamo myth" that she found so pernicious. The evidence of a rich multicultural and multiracial history of Texas exists, though we often have to look beyond the walls of established archival collections to see it fully. We also have to be careful to look past the silences (and the caricatures) in the narratives and the visual images that too easily come to hand, so that our own narratives do not perpetuate their distortions.

As we consider the impact of the past on the present through historical narratives, we come to the fourth moment: the *delivery* of the facts. Trouillot calls this "the moment of retrospective significance" because it has as much to do with the *consumption* of history as with its production. In other words, what is the audience prepared to take away from a given work of history? When the de la Peña diary was finally published in English in 1975, relatively few people got past the firestorm over "how Davy died" to appreciate the rest of the story. "De la Peña's war" was largely viewed through the narrow lens of Texas myth. Historians who defended the diary, claiming that it had indeed been published in 1836, had apparently not read the text closely enough to notice the 1838 reference that triggered Bill Groneman's skepticism. Groneman himself focused so intently on the single passage dealing with Crockett that he could dismiss the rest of the text as an elaborate "cover" created as a vehicle for a controversial hoax. For all the hoopla about the famous "de la Peña diary," the voice of the man himself was strangely silent—virtually lost—as his narrative of a tragic campaign reached the public.

Perhaps the only historical controversy to emerge from the Texas Revolution that could rival the "Death of Davy"—in terms of public fascination, mythic distortion, and the silencing of the authentic past—is the "Legend of the Yellow Rose." Though the story didn't break out of the archives until the 1950s, within a few years almost every Texan had heard of the beautiful slave girl, Emily, who seduced Santa Anna in his tent at San Jacinto, thus causing the lack of preparedness in the Mexican camp that gave the outnumbered rebels their lopsided victory, and Texas its independence.

Many salacious and utterly fictional details were added as newspaper columnists, after-dinner speakers, and popular writers embellished the story, but there was only one source for the tale, and it was very succinct. It came from the pen of William Bollaert (1807–1876), a British sojourner in the Republic of Texas who, fortunately for historians, was a compulsive writer and sketcher. Bollaert's thousands of manuscripts were eventually obtained by the "lumber king" and philanthropist Edward E. Ayer, who in turn donated them to Chicago's Newberry Library.

For most of the first half of the twentieth century, historians of the Texas Republic could be divided into those who had, and those who had not, made the trip north to see for themselves the rich Bollaert manuscripts, which included a daily journal of his extensive travels in Texas from 1842 to 1844. In 1956 this journal was published as *William Bollaert's Texas*, edited by W. Eugene Hollon.

On July 7, 1842, a ship carrying Bollaert from Galveston to Houston made the turn from the San Jacinto River into Buffalo Bayou. "We gazed with some interest," he wrote "at the battle field at San Jacinto." And then Bollaert added a comment that Hollon rendered as the following footnote:

> The Battle of San Jacinto was probably lost to the Mexicans, owing to the influence of a Mulatto Girl (Emily) belonging to Colonel Morgan, who was closeted in the tent with General Santana at the time the cry was made "the enemy! they come! they come!" and detained Santana so long, that order could not be restored readily again.

(It should be noted that Santa Anna had captured and burned the plantation of Colonel James Morgan, at Morgan's Point on

Galveston Bay, just a day or two before arriving at Lynch's Ferry, where he found Sam Houston's rebel army waiting for him.)*

At the moment that Bollaert's "fact" was delivered to the public, the popular song leader Mitch Miller was bringing back into popularity a minstrel song from the 1850s titled "The Yellow Rose of Texas." Despite the utter lack of evidence that this song had anything to do with the woman who was soon being called "The Maid of Morgan's Point," a lot of people added up two and two and got five: the mulatto maid *must* have been a slave (and therefore taken the name of her master), and she *must* have been "The Yellow Rose of Texas."

Today the high-rise building immediately north of the Alamo is known as the Emily Morgan Hotel, and a plaque in the lobby dedicated to the Yellow Rose of Texas claims that: "Were it not for the heroics of the beautiful mulatto slave Emily Morgan, Texas may to this day have remained Coahuilla y Texas [*sic*], Republic of Mexico. . . . Santa Anna's eye for women and Emily Morgan's allegiance to Texas proved to be a fatal combination for Mexico."

Holly Brear has examined at length the multiple messages about race, sex, and masculinity conveyed by this aspect of the

---

*As *Sleuthing the Alamo* was going to press, Texas reseacher Jeff Dunn discovered and brought to my attention the fact that Eugene Hollon was not the first to publish Bollaert's story of the woman in Santa Anna's tent. Hollon's close friend Joe B. Frantz slipped the racy vignette from the Bollaert papers into a footnote in his 1951 biography *Gail Borden: Dairyman to a Nation*, where it apparently eluded widespread popular notice. The same note appeared in Frantz's 1948 University of Texas Ph.D. dissertation on Borden, who was an early Texas newspaperman before his invention of condensed milk made him rich and famous. Santa Anna captured and destroyed Borden's printing press at Harrisburg just days before his troops swept through Morgan's Point on the way to San Jacinto.

Texas creation myth, focusing on the notion of both Mexicans and blacks as sensual beings, inferior to the more rational and disciplined white men who came to dominate them both. However, while a horde of modern mythmakers were at work elaborating the legend over the last half-century, a few historians were tying to find the "real" Emily.

Although writer Martha Anne Turner was guilty of considerable sensationalism and embellishment herself, she was the first to make the connection, in the 1970s, between the woman in Bollaert's note and Emily D. West, a "Free Negro" who had years earlier been identified as such by local historians in Houston from her 1837 passport application. The application to leave the Republic of Texas for New York was written for Emily by the Houston magistrate Isaac D. Moreland, who had been an artillery officer at the Battle of San Jacinto. He had added a very interesting note to the application, to the effect that this woman had lost her "free papers" at San Jacinto in April of 1836.

By the time of the sesquicentennial celebration of the battle in April 1986, Houston historian Margaret Swett Henson was able to sort out enough fact from fiction to tell the readers of *Texas Highways* magazine that Emily D. West (if not Emily Morgan) was "the Real Thing." Henson revealed one piece of information missing from Hollon's footnote: that Bollaert had obtained the story of Emily's presence in Santa Anna's tent from a veteran of the Battle of San Jacinto. But there was more to this story than even Henson realized.

In the late 1990s, Jim Lutzweiler, one of my graduate students, chanced to see a copy of Martha Anne Turner's book on the Yellow Rose on my shelf, and he began to explore the relationship between the evidence and the legend. Fascinated, he made it the subject of his term paper for my graduate seminar. As the students from the class gathered at my house for a holiday meal at the end of the semester, Jim and I exchanged Christmas presents that recalled the irony of O. Henry's "The Gift of the Magi." Each of us surprised the other with identical copies of a document that had recently surfaced in Texas. Mine came from Margaret Henson, his from the Rosenberg Library in Galveston, though neither of these sources possessed the original.

That document was held (and still is at this writing) by a bank that had obtained a trove of James Morgan documents in a loan foreclosure. Jeff Dunn, a Houston attorney well known for his expertise on early Texas history, had been called in to help determine the value of what appeared to be some of Morgan's business papers. Morgan, it seems, had arranged to bring several free blacks from the United States to work on his Texas plantation and mercantile business. Dunn's mundane task took on a whole new meaning when he recognized the name of a woman from New Haven, Connecticut, on a contract drawn up by Morgan in New York City in the autumn of 1835: Emily D. West.

It was a contract of indenture, under which West would come to Mexican Texas with Morgan as a cook and housekeeper for a year, to be paid in cash at the end of her term. Because of the bank's legal position, Jeff had to keep his discovery under wraps for almost five years, but in the late 1990s word of the document's existence was spreading among historians and archivists in the Houston area. With this new document in hand, my student Jim Lutzweiler was now so obsessed with Emily's story that he decided to make it the subject of his master's thesis.

Jim found vaguely familiar the name of a person who had signed the Morgan-West labor contract as a witness. It turned out to be Simeon Jocelyn, a leading New Haven philanthropist and abolitionist, who was active in charities benefitting the city's free black population. Jocelyn is perhaps best known to American historians for his efforts, in concert with his brother Nathaniel, in behalf of the *Amistad* captives—African victims of criminal slave traders—who were freed by the United States Supreme Court after their case was pled by ex-President John Quincy Adams in 1841. Was there a connection between Simeon Jocelyn and Emily D. West? His name was on none of the other Morgan labor contracts.

Before her death, Margaret Henson had tried without success to find Emily in the federal census for New Haven. In 1830 there was a free black couple with the last name of West, but other records showed that they had married in 1825 and the woman's name was Jane. The census showed no children in their home. When I found myself in New Haven for a Yale reunion a couple of years later, I tried a different search technique. Though only heads of households were listed by name in the 1830 census, a mark was made for every person in each place of residence according to the individual's age, sex, and status—the latter denoted by white, slave, or free black. One of the free black females so listed in New Haven was between the ages of ten and twenty-four, living with seven "whites" in household headed by Simeon S. Jocelyn.

Was the young woman of color living with the Jocelyn family in 1830 the "Yellow Rose of Texas"? I think so, but I can't prove it. Efforts to find a trace of her in the Jocelyn family papers have so far come up empty. But Jim Lutzweiler did make one more stunning find before he finished his master's thesis. When he went to the Newberry Library to examine for himself the Bollaert papers, Jim found that the "Emily" story had been cut out of one page and pasted onto another. The passage had also been marked "Private" by Bollaert. It took Lutzweiler two more visits to Chicago to find the notebook containing the damaged page from which the story had been cut, but it was worth the effort. When he found the matching pieces, they revealed that the San Jacinto veteran from whom Bollaert got the information was none other than General Sam Houston!

Bollaert cited, without mentioning its date, a letter from Houston to a friend as the source of the story of the woman in Santa Anna's tent. Sam Houston, of course, was the most renowned man in the Republic of Texas. Emily D. West was on the other end of the scale of fame and status. And yet Houston was able to identify her name, her employer, her racial status, and her presence on the battlefield in April of 1836—all of which have been corroborated by independent documentation. Though a decade ago Texas military historian Stephen L. Hardin could say that "there is not a scintilla of primary evidence to support the oft-repeated myth that Santa Anna was engaged in a tryst with mulatto slave girl Emily Morgan," there is enough new evidence not only to correct his details but also to suggest that there may be more to this story than myth.

But in the meantime, where is Emily? Will she ever be the subject of an authentic "moment of retrospective significance"? When Santa Anna swept down upon the Morgan plantation, Emily West became an eyewitness to the same revolution that was seen first-hand by Herman Ehrenberg and José Enrique de la Peña. The fact that we do not have *her* narrative is, of course, no simple accident of documentary disappearance. That she remains silent today is in large part a consequence of the dictates of race, class, and gender that kept her effectively silenced during her own lifetime. Were it not for the titillating tale that brought her presence in history to the attention of the public in the 1950s, would we even know that she existed? It is possible that we may still find her voice, but if we do, it is likely to be in a deeply hidden transcript.

That so many transcripts of the Texas Revolution have been so deeply hidden is one reason that I chose to write this book in such a personal fashion. Historians prefer, most of the time, to tell their stories as hidden, omniscient narrators. They focus the reader's attention not on themselves but on the objects of their investigation. Yet Trouillot has shown how difficult it is to separate the tellers of the tale from the tale itself—and the making of history from the production of it.

Those omniscient narrators are usually drawn to their subjects by personal histories not always obvious and infrequently revealed. Yet their own histories inevitably influence the way they do the telling, just as the circumstances of Ehrenberg or de la Peña influenced their production of history. I was shaped at an early age by both the myths and the realities of Texas, and the life that I once lived there has always resonated in the historical puzzles that keep pulling me back.

Thus it may be appropriate to tell one more Texas story: that of another young woman of color who suffered erasure through an act of silencing. When I began working on this book three years ago, my mother was still alive; but she died suddenly in August of 2002, before I had a chance to ask her help in finding the photograph of our family "Comedy" that I described in detail in the prologue. It was the picture taken so many years ago in the farmhouse basement: me in my cowboy outfit, my cousin Charlie standing in his underwear, and Gwendolyn, the black girl looking clearly embarrassed at the entire scene. The strenuous efforts of my sister and I to locate it after my mother's death were in vain. But I did recall my mom telling me she had made a copy for Charlie, too.

Charlie had no recollection of any such picture, and his widowed mother had passed away a year before my own. But after I described the photograph to him, and why I wanted it, he too was eager to find it. Having rummaged through almost every box of family memorabilia kept in his parents' old house, he called me one Saturday to tell me the bad news—there was no such picture to be found.

When he called back an hour later, I could tell by the tone of his voice that he had found something more important and surprising than the picture we had both been looking for. Or to be precise, he had found something more—and something less.

One last, overlooked shoebox held the picture taken of him and me and Gwendolyn in 1952. But Gwendolyn was nowhere to be seen. There were only the two of us standing there, in the clothes I had described to him. He turned over the photo and discovered, on the reverse side, that my mother had penned a note when she sent it along. Now, part of the note was missing—which explained Gwendolyn's absence. Someone had cut away the side of the photograph bearing her image. If it had not been for my memory and Charlie's diligence, I would have never seen the picture again, and Charlie would have never realized its meaning.

What is its meaning? I will make no guess as to the motives of whoever wielded the scissors. For whatever reason, only two of the three children in the cellar were to be remembered. After all, they were family. But Charlie tells me that Gwendolyn and her parents—tenant farmers on his family's land—were an important part of his young life. Her mother often shared her cooking with Charlie at lunchtime in their home on the farm; Gwendolyn's father extended to Charlie his rich knowledge of animals and plants and how to make them thrive.

Jim Crisp and Charlie Crisp, 1952.   (Courtesy Charles R. Crisp.)

This little piece of a picture is, in the end, a telling metaphor for the unrealized losses that we can suffer from a silenced past, from voices now lost. Even when it is "the other" who is silenced, we lose a part of our history—a part of ourselves—and a part of our family.

RECOMMENDATIONS FOR FURTHER READING

BACKGROUND AND CONTEXT

Barker, Eugene C. *The Life of Stephen F. Austin, Founder of Texas, 1793–1836: A Chapter in the Westward Movement by the Anglo-American People*. Nashville and Dallas: Cokesbury Press, 1926. Reprint, Austin: University of Texas Press, 1969.

Campbell, Randolph B. *Gone to Texas: A History of the Lone Star State*. New York: Oxford University Press, 2003.

Montejano, David. *Anglos and Mexicans in the Making of Texas, 1836–1986*. Austin: University of Texas Press, 1987.

Tijerina, Andrés. *Tejanos and Texas Under the Mexican Flag, 1821–1836*. College Station: Texas A&M University Press, 1994.

Weber, David J. *The Mexican Frontier, 1821–1846: The American Southwest Under Mexico*. Albuquerque: University of New Mexico Press, 1982.

Winders, Richard Bruce. *Crisis in the Southwest: The United States, Mexico, and the Struggle over Texas*. Wilmington, DE: Scholarly Resources, 2002.

ESSENTIAL INTERPRETATIONS OF THE TEXAS REVOLUTION

Hardin, Stephen L. *Texian Iliad: A Military History of the Texas Revolution*. Austin: University of Texas Press, 1994.

Lack, Paul D. *The Texas Revolutionary Experience: A Political and Social History, 1835–1836*. College Station: Texas A&M University Press, 1992.

PERSONALITIES

Cantrell, Gregg. *Stephen F. Austin: Empresario of Texas*. New Haven and London: Yale University Press, 2001.

Davis, William C. *Three Roads to the Alamo: The Lives and Fortunes of David Crockett, James Bowie, and William Barret Travis*. New York: HarperCollins, 1998.

de la Peña, José Enrique. *With Santa Anna in Texas: A Personal Narrative of the Revolution*. Translated and edited by Carmen Perry. Introduction by James E. Crisp. Expanded ed. College Station: Texas A&M University Press, 1997.

de la Teja, Jesús F., ed. *A Revolution Remembered: The Memoirs and Selected Correspondence of Juan N. Seguín*, 2d ed. Austin: Texas State Historical Association, 2002.

Haley, James L. *Sam Houston*. Norman: University of Oklahoma Press, 2002.

Jackson, Jack, ed. *Almonte's Texas: Juan N. Almonte's 1834 Inspection, Secret Report, and Role in the 1836 Campaign*. Austin: Texas State Historical Association, 2003.

CONTROVERSIES

Groneman, Bill. *Death of a Legend: The Myth and Mystery Surrounding the Death of Davy Crockett*. Plano, TX: Republic of Texas Press, 1999.

Lindley, Thomas Ricks. *Alamo Traces: New Evidence and New Conclusions*. Forward by Stephen Harrigan. Lanham, MD: Republic of Texas Press, 2003.

Roberts, Randy, and James S. Olson. *A Line in the Sand: The Alamo in Blood and Memory*. New York: The Free Press, 2001.

MYTH, MEANING, AND METHODOLOGY

Brear, Holly Beachley. *Inherit the Alamo: Myth and Ritual at an American Shrine*. Austin: University of Texas Press, 1995.

Flores, Richard R. *Remembering the Alamo: Memory, Modernity, and the Master Symbol*. Austin: University of Texas Press, 2002.

Gaddis, John Lewis. *The Landscape of History: How Historians Map the Past*. New York and Oxford: Oxford University Press, 2002.

Scott, James C. *Domination and the Arts of Resistance: Hidden Transcripts*. New Haven and London: Yale University Press, 1990.

Trouillot, Michel-Rolph. *Silencing the Past: Power and the Production of History*. Boston: Beacon Press, 1995.

RECENT ADDITIONS TO THE LITERATURE OF THE TEXAS REVOLUTION

Brands, H. W. *Lone Star Nation: How a Ragged Army of Volunteers Won the Battle for Texas Independence—and Changed America*. New York: Doubleday, 2004.

Davis, William C. *Lone Star Rising: The Revolutionary Birth of the Texas Republic*. New York: The Free Press, 2004.

Dimmick, Gregg J. *Sea of Mud: The Retreat of the Mexican Army after San Jacinto, An Archeological Investigation*. Austin: Texas State Historical Association, 2004.

Moore, Stephen L. *Eighteen Minutes: The Battle of San Jacinto and the Texas Independence Campaign*. Dallas: Republic of Texas Press, 2004.

Winders, Richard Bruce. *Sacrificed at the Alamo: Tragedy and Triumph in the Texas Revolution*. Abilene, TX: State House Press, 2004.